Hunting Grounds: Dogmen of the Lakes

Aaron Deese

Hunting Grounds:
Dogmen of the Lakes

This edition published by Small Town
Monsters Publishing, LLC in 2024

Copyright © 2024 by Small Town
Monsters Publishing, LLC

Author: Aaron Deese
Cover Artist: Jonathan Dodd

Table of Contents

Dedication

For my wife, Sara, who remains married to me despite my insistence that werewolves are real.

For Grandma Irene, whose stories laid the foundation for this work long before I knew that real werewolves were a thing.

For my son, Ezra. Everything will always be for you.

Acknowledgments

There are many, many people to thank for the creation of this book.

My parents, siblings, and in-laws, who have supported and believed in my ability to write books for as long as they've known me and helped keep Ezra happy when his dad was deep in the "writing process."

Heather, Seth and everyone else who has contributed to the life of Small Town Monsters Publishing, for taking a chance on a weird guy from the internet with not one, but now two outlandish manuscripts.

The various researchers, investigators, writers and colleagues who were interviewed to bring this work to life and are named throughout its chapters. It would not exist without the roads they paved.

The artists, Jonathan Dodd and Brett Marcus Cook, who helped give the things in my head visual life in this volume.

And finally, the witnesses who demonstrate unfathomable courage by admitting to the rest of the world that they have glimpsed the inexplicable, both in this and all other paranormal phenomena. It is for them that the work should be done, and because of them that it can be done at all.

Foreword (Forewoof)

When Aaron and I started this journey together regarding the subject of Dogman, I purposefully attempted to step away from any preconceived notions as to what I thought Dogman was. He had already done a much deeper dive than I ever had into everything about them, including their earliest known sightings, physical attributes, and commonalities in behavior and locations. This became incredibly apparent very early on during our trip to Texas, so I knew I really needed to buckle up for Kentucky. Having already been a fan of Aaron's *Hey Strangeness* podcast, I knew he had also been bitten by the need-to-know bug. He'd covered witches, skinwalkers, and even gnomes.

Open-mindedness would be plentiful between the two of us and would come in incredibly handy the more witnesses we'd talk to.

When we filmed our first documentary together, I had already spoken to many people on my show, *iNTO THE FRAY* who had seen or had a full-blown encounter with a Dogman. Where they were sighted varied greatly, from deep in the woods to confidently walking right up to the front porch. Opinions from these witnesses on what Dogman is varied as much as the sightings themselves. The only thing I knew for certain was that these creatures were nearly without fail, attached to a negative experience. They inhabit the same woods we frequently venture into for a relaxing hike, that memorable family camping trip, or the photo op with known tenants.

Aaron gets into much more than just the sighting itself though, including how it made the person feel afterward. How did it change their daily life, their sleep...did it find them moving to a desert landscape where running into one of these things should be far less likely? Did they hear the popping of joints, see huge glowing eyes, or hear a low growl...did this intensify their experience? Make it simply impossible to deny what they saw? Once we ask these types of questions, you can see the person shift uncomfortably in their seat while they relive the encounter. It may even pry a recollection of a detail loose they had forgotten to protect their own sanity.

Possible government cover-ups, mysterious disappearances and deaths, unclassifiable high-strangeness, and unique cryptid sightings run rife in the Land Between the Lakes. Even those who have had a terrifying experience will venture back out, consumed with a desire to know. Standing in the dark woods with Martin Groves while he recounts his encounters would be enough to make anyone a believer. His drive and curiosity are something that I know Aaron and I related heavily with. Each time we got in the car after an interview, there was some silence before discussing what we'd just learned or postulating what it may mean for the Dogman subject on the whole.

Many of the other well-known paranormal hot spots boast an impressive list much like the LBL. The reasoning behind why the LBL is so active will be heavily explored here. Do people with ill-intent, combined with special abilities, have the power to conjure an entity, or curse the land for all time? Does the natural landscape act as a beacon for the other side, making it an ideal playground for every player on team fifth dimension?

Besides the Werewolves...the outright paranormal anomalies that have also accompanied an encounter with one cannot be ignored. Much like many Bigfoot sightings, Dogman itself seems to have a few unique friends that enjoy tagging along. Some of the witnesses in this book will attest to that, because apparently a Dogman sighting alone wouldn't be brownie points enough in the nope category.

The complete and utter dread and evil felt by witnesses is a theme you will also find carried throughout, which only adds to the ultimate question when it comes to Dogman. Is this common narrative a primal fight or flight response from a flesh and blood apex predator kicking in, or something even deeper, such as a spiritual knowing that a very dark entity is in our presence? To be honest, either option would be equally fascinating.

This book and the evidence presented within will have you floundering from one conclusion to the other. Is this a breathing, breeding canid or is it something from another dimension that relishes the terror it can impart with simply a glimpse? Either way, I look forward to the next time Aaron and I can run with the wolves.

Shannon LeGro
iNTO THE FRAY RADIO

1
Beginnings

It is 1963, and it is a watershed year for the United States of America.

'63 would see Martin Luther King Jr.'s historic March on Washington, one of the most powerful events of the civil rights movement. Dr. King would deliver his landmark *I Have a Dream* speech to an assemblage of a quarter million people, imprinting his immortal words and undying vision upon human history.

Astronaut L. Gordon Cooper, an enthusiast of archaeology, would make a thirty-four hour and twenty-minute trip into outer space aboard the craft Faith 7, orbiting planet Earth 22 times. We would land on the moon only six years later, and this achievement would prove a critical steppingstone to our lunar pilgrimage.

Marilyn Monroe would pass away only a few months prior, losing her life in August of 1962 due to an apparent overdose.

The Vietnam War would continue to rage, over ten years before its eventual end. At the conclusion of hostilities with the Viet Cong, some would remark that America had lost its first war.

President Kennedy would lose his life in Dallas, TX, an event which would lead to decades of speculation and conspiracy theories. Names like "Dealey Plaza," "Jack Ruby" and "Lee Harvey Oswald" would become immortal overnight.

It was a time when societal norms were in flux, science was on a literal upward trajectory, and political strife would rock the boat of the American dream.

But other events, perhaps overshadowed by these and other contemporary bombshells, would transpire in the American heartland that would forever alter the course of life for thousands of US citizens.

From Rivers to Lakes

Before his untimely death, President Kennedy would sign a bill which would eventually lead to the creation of a national park comprising 170,000 of acres on the Tennessee/Kentucky border - 171,280 acres, for specificity's sake. Why this was done is a matter of debate, but newspaper articles reveal that plans were in motion to convert the area into a wilderness recreational zone as early as the 1920s. One headline published on August 23rd of 1924 by the News-Democrat out of Paducah, Kentucky reads, "'In Between the Rivers' Is Fine Region For Game Preserve.'" This section of land was rich in forest and fauna; but problematically, this land was also occupied by human residents.

Through extensive damming which would lead to the formation of the Barkley and Kentucky Lakes, The Land Between the Rivers, as it had been known, was no more. The inhabitants were displaced to the tune of approximately 900-2,000 families (depending on the account one references), despite their protestations. Some refused to leave. Eminent domain was invoked by the Tennessee Valley Authority, and in a few short months ancestral lands which had been held for generations became government property.

Homes were washed away. Town main streets became lake bottoms. Cemeteries were submerged and many forgotten. Stories began to pop up of residents' homes bulldozed and razed, their possessions still inside. Some were allegedly jailed for refusing to give up their land, and even the final holdouts were eventually driven away from the only homes they've ever known.

Today, this man-made peninsula is known as the Land Between the Lakes.

The Residents

The displaced residents of the newly renamed Land Between the Lakes were not recent arrivals but were the descendants of settlers dating back centuries. Many of these early settlers were led by American folk hero and frontiersman Daniel Boone, whose exploits are well documented by actual historians and not just meager paranormal researchers (like me). Boone worked for a man named Richard Henderson, who formed what would become the Transylvania Company in 1774, originally called the Louisa Company. Boone would scout locations for settlements and assist their new occupants in setting up shop, eventually establishing many of the homesteads of The Land Between the Rivers.

Pre-LBL, it was the setting of a rural lifestyle, populated primarily by farmers. Families worked the land together, reminiscent of the old days of the American frontier, chopping wood, tending livestock, and carrying on the legacy of their earlier ancestors.

It was discovered in the 1800s that in addition to a rich table of wildlife, abundant timber, and ample running water, that the Land Between the Rivers was also home to an enormous iron deposit. Mining operations were established in 1840, and, for the next 72 years, thousands upon thousands of tons of iron were drawn from the land and floated down the rivers. Limestone was also readily found in the area and was mined with equal fervor. The resulting environmental fallout would irreparably alter the landscape, and later conservation efforts beginning in the 1930s were heavily focused on remediating these decades of mineral extraction.

Even before this, the land was a shared hunting ground used by many Native American tribes. While it was not known to be a permanent settlement of any native peoples, there remain to this day purported burial mounds in areas now frequented by hunters and campers. Like innumerable other parts of the country, the land was once used by the First Nations before later settlers came to claim it as their own.

Many of these topics will arise again later in this volume. Our purpose now is to set the stage.

The Park

The Land Between the Lakes, or the LBL as it is often abbreviated, contains over 300 miles of shoreline alone, which is longer than the length of the Grand Canyon itself. The trail system makes up over 500 miles and hosts approximately 1.5 million annual visitors. It is the largest inland peninsula in the United States, almost fifty miles in length. It is a hub of tourism and recreation, and is a prime destination for hunting, fishing, camping, hiking and even horseback riding.

The area is rich in wildlife. Birds, fish, land animals of all sorts (and perhaps a few spectral horrors) populate the park. Elk and Bison can be seen in herds and are a particular draw in the summer and fall. There are plenty of predatory species as well, including black bears and bobcats. Red wolves, which were long ago declared extinct as a native species, have been reintroduced through breeding and hybridization programs, resulting in a population of the animals which can be seen by visitors at the Woodlands Nature Station.

In 1939 the Kentucky Woodlands National Wildlife Refuge was established. New species were introduced to the area, including ospreys, otters, turkeys, and Canada geese. Bald eagles were also added, which are another popular attraction for visitors.

A perfectly innocuous national park, despite its checkered history, with nothing particularly fantastic to draw the speculative eye.

Or maybe not.

The Beast

When areas of high strangeness are mentioned, some locations are seemingly inseparable from the discussion. Point Pleasant, WV may be the most famous. Chestnut Ridge is another popular choice. Of course, who can forget Skinwalker Ranch and the Uinta Basin, the haunted streets of New Orleans, or the ghost/UFO/sasquatch riddled corridors of the Texas Dogman Triangle?

Weird in equal measure, and perhaps as famous as any of them, is the Land Between the Lakes. After hearing stories and rumors for years of strange creatures within the LBL's borders, I leapt at the opportunity to investigate them myself. What I found would subvert all my expectations, leading me down a literal and proverbial path of new questions and ancient lore.

Hundreds of hours of research, detailed conversations and old-fashioned speculation evolved into a two-day trip into the woods. I went to places I'd only read about, places that some say don't exist, and met with witnesses who knew for certain something I had only suspected:

Something lives in the Land Between the Lakes. *Something* which hitherto has defied proper classification. *Something* which has spawned rumors and campfire stories for a very long time. It is a thing which many in even the paranormal and cryptozoological communities are quick to dismiss. It makes very little sense within the realm of what we understand regarding the animal kingdom, and hints at stranger things than we are equipped to dissect. It is a creature far older than the LBL, storied and ancient, depicted since before we knew the Earth was round. Something our ancestors whispered of, with hints as to its nature left by even the oldest known human civilization.

They go by many names, but today we call them Dogmen. Some regard them as unclassified animals - cryptids, in our lexicon - which may be mutants, aberrant one-offs, or even an undiscovered species. Others will tell you that they are extra-terrestrial, genetic experiments, or spectral demons from beyond the veil of reality. Another common explanation is a sub-species of Sasquatch, perhaps a baboon-like offshoot, justifying the pointed ears and elongated snout that typify Dogman sightings. We must also give equal time to skepticism and assume that at least some encounter stories are the result of coyotes, dogs or even wolves being mistaken for a supranatural nightmare. This does not, of course, explain why the creatures walk upright, but we will discuss these specifics soon enough.

Whatever they are, an overwhelming pool of eyewitness testimony and a growing section of physical evidence may cement in the minds of many researchers an unsettling fact. A fact I am undeniably convinced of, and which we will explore throughout the duration of this volume. One which, after my own visit to the Land Between the Lakes, I find utterly inescapable.

Werewolves exist. They live in the Land Between the Lakes, and it's anyone's guess as to how long they have been there.

Together, and with care, we will journey deep into the Dogman's territory. We will walk between the trees of the park and explore some of its hidden reaches. We will hear from the witnesses who have encountered these inexplicable canines and learn the ways in which their lives have been irreparably altered. We will meet investigators who have hunted the hunters, pursuing impossible beings in a thirst for knowledge, and examine the evidence they have meticulously gathered.

It is here, in the words of Sondheim, that we journey into the woods.

It is here that we enter the Hunting Grounds.

2
Travel Log #1: Into the Woods

11/3/23
8:17 AM CST

The waters of Lake Barkley are still. My breath gouts steam into the frigid air; I can't tell the smoke of my Red 100 from the fog of my own lungs. There is no snow or ice, but my deep-southern blood is unaccustomed to the elements of Kentucky. My usual haunt of Central Texas is experiencing a prolonged, on-again-off-again summer, and this far north, I am cleanly out of my element.

The trees, tall on all sides and stretching the entirety of the bank, present a gray-brown wall of towering trunks, topped by the brown-orange-amber of autumn. There is little green amongst the canopy, at least in contrast to how it must look during the summer. I am told this is typical of the fall here, but that in the warmer months the brush cover is far denser.

I arrived twelve hours ago, fresh from a connecting flight between San Antonio and Atlanta. From there it was a 90-minute car ride from Nashville International Airport, courtesy of my colleague Eli Watson, and my investigative partner, Shannon LeGro. The flip-flopping time zones - Central to Eastern to Central again - might have threatened to throw off my circadian, but I awoke in a fresh and eager state. Fresh for the adventure promised by the next two days, and eager to get my feet on the ground. Eager to start hunting.

I don't actually hunt, not literally. It's never appealed to me enough to make the monetary and chronological commitments necessary to undertake it. I also don't like guns much.

My pursuit is of a different nature.

We arrived at roughly nine PM local time, met by the enthusiastic welcome of the Small Town Monsters film crew as we entered the short-term rental. The four-story, seven-bedroom, split-level lake house will spend the next two days serving as a film studio, research center, lounge, base of operations and much more besides. Cameras and lenses, laptops, memory cards, power cords, data cables and plenty of things I can't identify litter nearly every inch of the wooden dining room table.

I offload my own equipment, meager as it is, arranging my notebook, voice recorder, air pods and spare pens - all of which I will eventually misplace - next to my laptop on my room's bedside credenza. The furniture is white wicker, all matching, and reminds me of my late grandmother's retirement home. A few hours of fitful sleep, a zombie-like slog to the kitchen for a cup of coffee - brewed by Zac Palmisano before I got out of bed for the day - and I'm smoking a cigarette on the second story patio overlooking Lake Barkley.

The forest evokes feelings of calm and quiet. I note a recurring impulse to lay back on the incline of the grassy hill leading to the shore, but the hundreds of miles crossed to reach this place were not for the sake of leisure. Shannon and I have a job to do.

The woods seem to belie the nature of the thing, which is the purpose of our visit, almost as if they wish to conceal the horrors said to skulk within them.

We've come here in search of monsters. Time will tell if there are any to be found.

The Northwest shore of Lake Barkley, KY in 2023.
Photo by the author.

3
Strangeness In and Around

Dogman is far from the only uncanny aspect of the vaunted Land Between the Lakes. It would be enough, were the canine cryptid a singular aspect of strangeness within the park, to draw the attention of the paranormal community at large, but the LBL is not content with a single paranormal story for its already impressive resume. If one were to produce a Venn diagram of paranormal phenomena, then include the Land Between the Lakes as a central field, the crossover would be impressive to say the least. Elijah Henderson of the Cryptid Studies Institute, who has spent innumerable hours in the park, puts it well when he says,

"The Land Between the Lakes is special for those interested in strange phenomena in the way that no matter what you're interested in, more than likely there is something for you there. From numerous sightings of sasquatch, to reports of a bipedal wolf-like creature called a Dogman, to otherworldly supernatural frights, and even reports of UFOs have taken place not far from the park. Land Between the Lakes is a veritable cornucopia of oddities, and even the surrounding area is ripe with unusual sights and sightings of cryptid creatures."

Jeremiah Byron of *The Bigfoot Society Podcast*, one of my go-to-guys in the realm of the bizarre, offered this,

"The Land Between the Lakes seems to be a hotbed of strangeness. I'm not sure how I feel about it but if I ever get the chance to investigate it, I will be extremely aware of my surroundings."

This would prove useful advice during my own excursion.

It has been noted in many examinations of anomalous occurrences that they tend to take place near or adjacent to places with bizarre, sometimes unpleasant names. One example is the *Boca Del Infierno*, or Hell's Mouth, a 600-meter-deep former mineshaft which can be visited in Guanajuato, Mexico. Guanajuato has a strange and sometimes ghoulish history which includes ghosts, mummies, sightings of La Lechuza, a Latin-American shapeshifter, and serial killers. In the Land Between the Lakes, a popular hiking path named The Devil's Backbone is a part of the Fort Henry Trail System. Fort Henry is one of many allegedly haunted spots in the park, and the location of one of the many Dogman sightings chronicled in the books of Martin Groves (whom we will meet in short order).

Another Devil's Backbone, interestingly enough, is also found smack dab in the middle of the Texas Dogman Triangle, north of San Antonio near Canyon Lake. This winding road snakes through the shrubland of the Texas hill country and is said to be the location of many road fatalities. Spectral armies march in the area, the ghostly remnants of a bloody civil war battle, and its adjacency to both Dogman and Sasquatch sightings is of particular note. This is one of many synchronistic parallels between the Texas Dogman Triangle and the Land Between the Lakes that came to my attention during the drafting of this volume, but our focus lies with the latter.

Spooks and Spirits

"My boyfriend and I were camping in a place, and we got run out. There was something in the woods. It's haunted."

The preceding quote comes from an employee of a visitors' center in the Land Between the Lakes. It would be relayed to Jessi and Joe Doyle of Hellbent Holler during their exploration of the park, amidst filming *The Werewolf Experiments* series, available on YouTube.

Ghosts may be the most commonly reported and experienced paranormal event. Most cryptid sightings require a wooded or unpopulated area, and UFO encounters need an open sky. Hauntings can occur virtually anywhere, and when the bar for entry is set only as far as the perception of the experiencer, it likely comes as no surprise that reports of encounters with ghosts - auditory, visual, kinetic, and plain old feelings of being watched - can be found at nearly every point on most any map. The idea that Land Between the Lakes should be an exception seems an obvious misnomer.

A phantom truck driver is alleged to hang out on Highway 68-80 or, according to some accounts, the Dogman-encounter ladened Trace. Bright lights appear behind isolated motorists, tailgating them at an uncomfortably close proximity before eventually disappearing. The "phantom motorist" is yet another phenomenon we see repeated in other areas, and a topic worth investigating in its own right. The story behind the LBL's phantom motorist seems to concern a truck driver allegedly killed in an accident whose ghost now lingers in the area, though the driver's identity is an elusive detail. The pitch-dark and winding roads of the Land Between the Lakes are an imposing drive as it is, nevermind adding a spectral tailgater to the mix.

The book *Haunted Houses & Family Ghosts of Kentucky* by William Lynwood Montell contains several stories from Lyon and Trigg, the LBL's home counties in Kentucky, with one in particular adjacent to the Kentucky Dam.

The story, titled *The House with a Lantern* describes a long-abandoned house which, at midnight, sports a ghostly lantern in its window, accompanied by the sound of footsteps. The home's former occupant is supposed to have been a man who would, every night, walk the halls with a lantern in hand, and was found after death with the light at his side. A key detail in this tale is that the house is alleged to have been abandoned since the Kentucky Dam was built, hinting at yet another displaced resident of the Land Between the Rivers.

Many of the region's nearly 300 cemeteries are purported to be haunted, as is to be expected in any situation where nearly 300 cemeteries are to be found. One might reason that the entire park has the potential to be haunted, but this is better left as the topic of a different book.

Lights in the Sky

Uncanny aerial phenomena are nearly as commonly reported as interactions with spirits, and in a time when public discourse on the topic is probably the highest it's been since the 50s, it would be negligent not to at least make mention of it here.

Two major UFO incidents occurred in close proximity to the park. Two famous cases which set standards in the field of Ufology (Uapology?) and which are as famous in those circles as The Beast of Bray Road in the Dogman community.

Thomas Mantell - 1948

In 1948, Kentucky Air National Guardsman Thomas Mantell would report seeing a strange object while piloting a P-51 Mustang fighter craft. Mantell would pursue the object, which moved at speeds that should have been impossible for an aircraft of the day. Contact was lost with Mantell before he reached Franklin, Kentucky. It was here that his crashed plane was later recovered.

Franklin is only 90 miles from the Land Between the Lakes. Before Mantell chased the object towards Franklin, it was spotted by the control tower at Goddard Army Airfield, which is a part of Fort Knox, 170 miles from the park. Marking these points on a map - Goddard Airfield and Franklin, Kentucky - it immediately becomes evident that the subject of Mantell's pursuit was moving *in the direction of* the Land Between the Lakes. It is unknown what the object was, where it went or what its intentions were (if it had any) but continuing its known trajectory would have taken it west of Nashville over the southern end of Kentucky Lake, likely near Highway 70 or

Interstate 40. Kentucky Lake is, of course, one of the aquatic barriers that forms the LBL peninsula. This is only a cursory glance at the "Mantell Incident," as it is often called, and readers are encouraged to seek out the details of the story at their leisure. At time of writing, a new documentary titled *Lost Contact* featuring interviews with surviving relatives of Thomas Mantell is being produced by Small Town Monsters, slated for release in 2024.

The Goblins

The second of these two high-profile UFO incidents occurred in 1955. Over the Sutton family's farmhouse, a UFO sighting would light up the night sky, catching the attention of one family member who was outside collecting water. Immediately following the initial UFO sighting, the witness and several relatives encountered what they described as a "small man" with glowing yellow eyes, a large round head, long thin arms, and long pointed ears. The creature appeared surrounded by a bright glow. More of the creatures would appear in the windows of the house, on the roof, in trees and around other places on the property. The Sutton family opened fire on the creatures multiple times. When shot, the creatures would fall or stumble back. They also emitted a metallic sound on ballistic contact but were not killed. They were hit with buckshot and a .22 rifle. Police later arrived on the scene. While en route, the officers also witnessed UFO activity, which they described as "several meteors" that emitted a sound "like artillery" moving in a descending arc towards the Sutton house. The police considered that the witnesses might have been drinking but found no evidence to support this idea. Not to mention, the Suttons did not allow alcohol in the house. The police located a patch in the grass where one of the creatures had fallen when shot and noticed that it had a distinct glow when viewed from a specific angle. The police chief himself verified that there was a "stain" on the grass. Officers eventually left without seeing the creatures themselves, but the Suttons would have additional sightings throughout the night, with the final occurring just before sunrise.

This incident would occur in the Kelly/Hopkinsville area, only thirty miles from the border of the Land Between the Lakes.

And Many More

These are two very well-known incidents which regularly permeate UFO discussions, but they are a small drop in the bucket where Tennessee and Kentucky are concerned.

The NUFORC database (National UFO Reporting Center) has been in operation for 49 years at time of writing and contains over 170,000 individual sightings. Over 2,000 of those sightings took place in Tennessee, and nearly 1,700 of them are from Kentucky.
Sightings in both states would spike in October of 2022, coinciding with a particularly dramatic case that we will examine later on.

On Other Monsters

Human paths often cross with the world's most famous cryptid in The Land Between the Lakes. We refer, of course, to Sasquatch. There are reports which coincide with apparent Dogman activity, as well as plenty of sightings recorded both at night and in broad daylight. The phenomenon is so frequent that it warrants its own chapter within this volume and is thus explored in greater detail later on.

There are other cryptid sightings in the park as well or at least encounters that generally fit the definition. Dewey Edwards of the *Cryptids and Critters* research group relayed the story of a large lizard, perhaps three to five feet in length, which was found dead in the park and put on ice. Its present whereabouts are unknown.

Chatter amongst locals has also consisted of a strange creature known as The Wampus Cat for many years. The Wampus Cat is an odd slice of American folklore. It hangs out in the Appalachian reaches and is said to have roots in Cherokee traditions. Most often described as a human/cat hybrid with six legs (that's right, six) its origin is said to be the result of a woman donning the skin of a mountain lion and assuming some of its form.

Kentucky is home to additional legends of strange canines as well. The Kentucky Hellhound of Pike County was investigated by the production team of the popular Travel Channel show *Mountain Monsters*. Its first appearance is alleged to have taken place in 1939, and the *Mountain Monsters* team would claim to have captured it on film. Additional sources of information online regarding this creature are admittedly sparse.

During my own visit to the Land Between the Lakes I would hear anecdotes of Nessie-like river beasts, winged humanoids and other assorted creatures. Time constraints prevented me from pursuing these leads in any great detail, but they are mentioned here due to their relevance. Such a vast array of oddness exists in the LBL that Aleksandar Petakov would film the first episode of his series *Strange Places* during our visit, hitting on a number of points not mentioned in this volume. Shannon LeGro, my investigative partner during the trip, would offer an apt take during our post-visit interview.

"The resounding theme of the LBL is that many strange things go on, even outside the Dogman phenomena. Ghost lights, phantoms, possible Native American curses, gruesome murders and strange disappearances. Walking the woods in several locations during our time there, it's very easy to see how unsavory people and paranormal entities alike might utilize a prime opportunity to show off their darker side, while unsuspecting hikers and campers are attempting to mind their own."

We might spend countless hours, lines of text, and chapters digging into any one of these. In truth, I found it difficult to succinctly enumerate all the weird things happening around the park and stumbled upon plenty of other examples which might have warranted inclusion in this chapter. A full exploration is not possible within this volume but suffice to say that The Land Between the Lakes has a veritable buffet of options for the paranormal gourmand.

4
Dogman: A Profile

"Have you ever uncovered a story where the Dogman is actually having a good day? Because they all seem like they're having a terrible day."
Jeremiah Byron - Bigfoot Society Episode #374

While I, and many others, have been deeply immersed in the Dogman topic for varying numbers of years, it occurs to one that not everyone is familiar with the term or what it means. The fact is that its definition varies depending on the source of the answer, and like many cryptids and other paranormal phenomena, it may boast a legion of interpretations and concluding explanations. I am asked to comment on this question with some regularity, and my answer has evolved over time spent digging away at the history and nature of this bizarre entity.

At First Glance

We begin at the surface. A Dogman is a canine form that displays bipedal ambulatory locomotion. When I'm not trying to sound well read, it's a dog that walks on two legs.

The natural inclination which many of us feel, likely brought about by lifetimes immersed in pop culture, is that this description resembles a cinema-ready werewolf. That term - werewolf - is often used by witnesses in describing what they have seen, at a loss for how to better define it. It is for this reason that I, and others whom I will not speak for, use the terms werewolf and Dogman interchangeably. One also notes while writing a book on a particular topic that there are only so many ways to describe said topic, and variety of language is an important component of an engaging manuscript. We can only say "Dogman" so many times, and the term already appears in the title of this book, totaling well over 200 mentions.

The earliest mentions of "Dogman" in the modern cryptozoological lexicon come from the far north of the United States. Two cases would typify encounters with Dogman-like entities, displaying a profile that we see repeated in later reports. Much time has been spent by better minds than my own recording and recounting these cases, but a summary is in order.

The Michigan Dogman is one of these two. The earliest recorded sighting took place in 1887 in Wexford County, Michigan. Lumberjacks working in the area reported encountering an upright walking beast with uncannily person-like anatomy and the head of a dog or wolf, which issued bone chilling, human-like cries. It was also said to have striking blue eyes, which is an aspect of these stories - eye color - that seems to continually catch the attention of experiencers. Other potential encounters took place in the mid 19th century, and in 1987 area DJ Steve Cook wrote and produced a song called, "The Legend" chronicling alleged stories of the Dogman's activity. Cook produced the song as an April Fool's joke, but the radio station which aired the song was soon inundated with calls from Michigan residents claiming to have had encounters with the creature. Joke or not, the song prompted a bevy of unrelated witnesses - a paranormal enthusiast's dream - to come forward and vouch for the creature's existence.

Another case, The Beast of Bray Road, comes up in nearly every discussion one endeavors to have on the topic of Dogmen. Chronicled in detail in a series of newspaper articles, and later in a seminal book by the late Linda Godfrey, The Bray Road monster has become as much a part of the search for Dogman as discussion over what Dogman actually is.

The Beast would make its key appearances in Elkhorn, Wisconsin during the 80s and 90s. Motorists would report seeing a bipedal, hairy creature moving along the road - Bray Road specifically - and sightings from independent witnesses became a regular occurrence. It was seen to feed on roadkill, another repeating Dogman behavior. The creature's first appearance is said to have taken place in 1936, and almost a century later, it has become a staple part of the area's folklore.

Bray Road Today

Bray Road is also not a "dead" area of activity in the scope of this phenomenon. Research into the area is ongoing, and the strange sightings have not ceased. Some of my contemporaries have taken to investigating the continued legacy of the Bray Road Beast, and one examination would yield a mixed bag of seemingly paranormal evidence.

Eric Mintel is an award-winning jazz musician who has performed at the White House on two separate occasions, for presidents Clinton and Obama respectively. He has also played at, among innumerable other places, the United Nations. He is also the founder and chief of Eric Mintel Investigates, a paranormal investigative team. Their work has been licensed for television in multiple states, and the team continues to document bizarre paranormal occurrences across the county.

On October 3rd of 2021, Eric and his team traveled to Elkhorn, Wisconsin in search of the notorious Bray Road monster. Eric admits they approached the visit without any grand expectations.

"I went in thinking we were going to hear some great stories and talk to some cool folks but never thinking once that we would encounter this creature."

He then amends,

"But we did."

Eric and his team would run across several noteworthy items during their trip to Elkhorn. They spoke with witnesses who had recorded inexplicable tracks - large, unidentifiable, and made by something heavy. They would meet a man named Lee, who had been farming on his property since 2011. Lee would describe a raccoon discovered on his land which had been seemingly eviscerated - essentially dissected, its innards splayed about on the ground. Mutilations of cattle and other animals are often mentioned in potential Dogman encounters, but this would be only the tip of the iceberg for Lee. He would also report strange lights or orbs, more odd tracks, and an inexplicable mist that seemed to have no clear origin. All these incidents of High Strangeness are noted in other areas of apparent Dogman activity - including the Land Between the Lakes.

The team would interview additional witnesses, but their own experience provides the lynchpin of the investigation.

They would return to Lee's property at night and immediately began to experience strange electronic interference with their equipment. Shortly after, they would have what one can only equate to a UFO sighting, capturing footage of an oddly moving, flashing light in the sky above. Its nature remains a mystery, but the team did sight a recognizable plane at the same time, providing an easy point of reference to known aircraft.

A series of high-pitched howls were to follow. Audible in the video available online, the sound is decidedly canine. We're presented with the possible explanation that this is a dog or other known animal, but its adjacency to the aforementioned strangeness is an obvious note of interest. In addition, on-the-ground audio does not translate to YouTube without a loss of fidelity, and the seasoned investigative team were certain that the sound was not made by a coyote. The timing also cannot be accounted for, and Eric and crew would receive additional reports during their visit which seemed to indicate that this odd howling was not an isolated occurrence. They would personally experience three, and when I interviewed Eric in 2024, he would explain,

"And the howls, there were three. And that third one was what sounded to me like a man screaming, like a low, guttural, scream-growl-yell combo."

Eric would also state,

"That was the weirdest thing I've ever heard."

No small statement, particularly for an investigator with Eric's level of experience.

Next, a loud rustling sound was noted in the surrounding woods. Its source remains undetermined, but the volume and disbursement indicated to the team that there was more than one creature lurking in the forest. What's more, the rustling would be accompanied by something the team had learned of earlier that same day - a strange, unprecipitated mist, creeping slowly out of the trees. For those taking notes, remember this bit, as it is one of many pieces we will return to later on.

Then there would be a final clue - Eyeshine.

The camera would capture what very much appears to be a pair of eyes, glinting in the meager equipment lights beyond the wood line, and plainly visible in the video referenced for this summary.

All of this would occur in about ten minutes. The entire sequence of events, and accompanying interviews, can be seen in the

YouTube documentary *The Beast of Bray Road (Alive and Well)*, and it is recommended viewing to readers of this volume.

Repeating Patterns

Prior to Linda Godfrey's diligent chronicling of these cases, the Dogman was something not commonly discussed in cryptozoological circles. The search for the beast has received a shot in the arm in recent years, and Dogman has quickly climbed the ranks from an obscure concept barely removed from Hollywood to its own niche within the niche of those who hunt for unknown animals. Documentaries, podcasts, books - two of which I wrote - and whole organizations have homed in on the search for real-life werewolves in the intervening years.

Bray Road and Michigan are not the only noteworthy historical cases either. The Defiance Werewolf is known to have surfaced in Defiance, Ohio in 1972. A canine on two legs exceeding six feet in height would strike a railway worker with a piece of wood, which it apparently manipulated with some level of dexterity, employing its front/upper paws as hands. The man, Ted Davis, would encounter the creature again a few nights later, this time accompanied by a second witness. The creature would be sighted yet once more, this time by another party, and allegedly several additional reports were made to law enforcement before the activity petered out.

Texas has seen regular Dogman activity for a century or more, which I profiled in detail in my previous work, *The Texas Dogman Triangle*. One sighting in particular is a favorite of mine, which took place in Lockhart, Texas in 1980. A man named James Witter would witness a pair of large, canine-like creatures which he described as looking like hyenas. James, a seasoned cattleman, set out after the creatures on horseback, intent on lassoing one. Both animals bolted and outran James' horse at a dead sprint before leaping over a fence and disappearing into the woods. As James described it when I met him in October of 2022,

"I wasn't riding no dead-head horse."

James would have repeated sightings of the creatures in the days to come but would retreat from the public eye due to the sensational way in which the media covered the story. I was fortunate enough to meet James in October of 2022 and hear his saga firsthand while filming *The Dogman Triangle*.

An anecdote I enjoy is that "Once is a random event, twice is a coincidence, three times is a pattern."

I forget where I heard it - perhaps I made it up - but this thought continually rattles around in my head when I ponder the topic of werewolves. We can point to far more than three occurrences in every aspect of the Dogman encounters which are hitherto documented, save perhaps some odd qualities bleeding into the supernatural realm.

From the stories above and other sightings, a template for Dogman encounters has been derived and unofficially adopted by much of the paranormal community. I can hardly purport to speak for the public-at-large, but my own conversations and research have displayed a pattern of physical traits, behavior and witness responses that seem to personify appearances by these creatures.

Appearance

First to be discussed, and to leave its impression upon witnesses, is the creature's appearance. They are often seen to transition from a four-legged stance into a two legged one, or vice versa, shortly after being spotted by the witness reporting the encounter. What seems to catch the eye most often is the obvious - a dog walking on two legs. While this is represented in the known world of zoology - mutants, animals compensating for an injury or displaying a learned behavior - it is hardly common, and not a natural habit for most canine species.

The eyes are another feature commonly remarked upon, as mentioned. The Michigan Dogman's eyes were said to be blue, while the Bray Road Beast sported eyes of amber yellow. Yellow may be the most commonly repeated eye color, but we can also find tales of red, black and white respectively from across the United States. Some reports indicate that the eyes display typical animal eyeshine, while a considerable portion of others describe glowing independent of any light source.

The creatures display an abundance of fur, sometimes described as shaggy, but are also cited as having thin hair and visible skin. Once again, we can cite the Michigan Dogman, as well as another case in Texas circa 1957 out of the town of Greggton. The creature is not often said to have a tail, though I have encountered descriptions which include it. Generally, tails are described as short and furry, like that of a bobcat.

Teeth and claws, when visible, are generally described as prominent and sharp. Once again in both Texas and Wisconsin, reports include Dogmen leaving long gouge marks on window screens and even the hoods of cars. Odd markings have been documented on trees within the LBL as well, demonstrated by Hellbent Holler's recent excursions into the area.

Lastly, but among the most important, are the facial features. There are many in this field of research who believe Dogman encounters to be mistaken run-ins with Sasquatch, and while I believe there is validity to this idea, I am unconvinced that it covers the whole of the werewolf question. Witnesses unequivocally describing a "werewolf" sighting will without fail mention an elongated muzzle and pointed ears - two features which are decidedly not common in the primate world. Some apes do display them, such as baboons, but they are more often the traits of a canine. It must also be considered that many descriptive sightings of Dogmen take place in near or full daylight, further cementing the eyewitness descriptions of "werewolf." Another anecdote which has often been relayed is that they appear "like Anubis," of ancient Egyptian mythology. Anubis's canine head is likely based on that of a jackal, with prominent ears and a long snout.

In addition, one must consider the amount of conviction a witness must feel regarding what they've seen such that it prompts them to use the term "werewolf," when one could easily claim to have seen a Sasquatch as a more likely descriptor. At least Sasquatch sightings are generally regarded as something which takes place in the real world, even if one does not believe in the phenomenon itself.

A composite Dogman sketch based on eyewitness descriptions. Art by Brett Marcus Cook

Behavior

The behavior of these creatures may be their most frightening component, and one which further separates them from the Bigfoot phenomenon. Sasquatches are often described as curious, not friendly, but not usually aggressive. There are plenty of aggressive Bigfoot encounters, to be sure, but even a fifty-fifty split doesn't approach the overwhelming percentage of unfriendly personas described in Dogman's odd history. We will return to the "Sasquatch question" at a more appropriate time.

They are frequently seen to stare down human witnesses, displaying a behavior which we recognize as an intimidation or dominance tactic in known canines. Teeth are sometimes barred, and eyewitness sketches often feature a snarling, grin-like sneer.

They seem to move about with a perceivable lack of fear, at least with regard to human beings, and have been known to stalk and even charge at human targets. In numerous examples of cases I've researched, the witnesses will describe being followed or even harassed before catching sight of the subject in question, and this behavior seems to be especially prominent on the Tennessee/Kentucky border.

In addition, they display hostility towards domestic dogs. Anecdotes of Dogmen attacking and even consuming pets and cattle dogs can be found across the map, including in the Land Between the Lakes, which may be a further indication that their activity is that of a flesh and blood animal. They are frequently noted near large bodies of water and ample tree coverage - both of which the LBL has in abundance - and seem to prefer areas rich in natural game. As mentioned previously, the preserve is home to a vast roster of indigenous and introduced animal species which would provide a cornucopia of options to the enterprising predator. There are no Dogman encounters I am aware of which describe them as vegetarian, and numerous in which they seem to feed on both roadkill and large animals. Livestock mutilation, once again, is another recurring aspect of their appearances.

Some reports, though they are admittedly fewer in number, indicate that these are creatures that travel in packs or pairs, some even indicating complex family systems. We must once again reference the story of James Witter and the Beast of Plum Creek, as well as a potential encounter with a hunting pair in the LBL by Jessi and Joe Doyle (Chapter 8). Their research has laid much of the foundation upon which this book was conceived, and we will hear more from them throughout our exploration.

I asked Shannon LeGro for her take on this phenomenon overall, and she provided this response.

"The Dogman subject has always fascinated me because it's such a unique creature. By all rights, it shouldn't be something anyone has ever seen. A 'werewolf' that walked in on its hocks right out of your favorite horror flick. And a grumpy one at that. Feelings of dread, joints popping, confident, and in your face. Dogman is on a very short list of things that people over the years have told me without fail...they never want to see one again."

The Next Steps

The tone of this volume will be predicated on the notion that these beings do, in fact, exist. If repeated eyewitness encounters across the country are to be given any credence - and in my mind, they should be - then to continue to tow a line of abject skepticism is a course I can no longer assume. Equal consideration will be given to a variety of explanations, but the fact remains that these people, *unequivocally*, have seen *something* they could not understand. Very often, these people are seasoned hunters and outdoorsmen, with collective centuries of experience in wild places and in dealing with wild animals. Despite their backgrounds, they continue to report the same thing.

Upright walking canines. Werewolves. Dogmen.

5
Werewolves Most Ancient

From the French

Perhaps the earliest piece of literature devoted specifically to the werewolf was penned in 1865 by minister and author Sabine Baring-Gould. Baring-Gould became fascinated with the topic after an incident in France prompted him to question the reality of what he had previously considered to be a mere story. A prolific writer and folklorist, with over 1200 works in his bibliography, his interests ran the gamut from outrageous tales of otherworldly beings to academic essays, plays, hymns and a variety of others.

Baring-Gould was visiting Vienne, France, home to a Druidic ruin known as the *Pierre Labie*, which is still accessible to this day. When he learned of the relic's existence, he deviated from his previous plans to make time to pay it a visit, devoting a day to examining and sketching the old pile of gray stones. He was late in beginning his journey home and found himself readily stranded in the French countryside without transport beyond his own feet. After a ten-mile walk, he was on the outskirts of a small hamlet, wherein he located a priest who spoke French and with whom he could communicate (many people in France spoke Occitan, a variety of romance languages and other non-French dialects at the time). The priest offered to shelter Gould for the evening, but our hero was intent on returning to his family before retiring.

From *The Book of Werewolves*:

Out spoke then the mayor; "Monsieur can never go back tonight across the flats, because of the, the," and his voice dropped; "the loups-garoux"

This term - *Loups Garoux* - translates almost directly from French into "Wolf Man." Any research into the history of werewolves leads one down a direct path to stories of the *Loups Garoux*, later adapted to Rougarou, by French settlers in the North American South. The beast is known to haunt the bayous of Louisiana and will arise again later in our exploration of The Land Between the Lakes.

Baring-Gould was insistent upon leaving the hamlet that night, and it was said that he must be escorted across the flats to ensure his safety. One of the assembled peasants would then interject. The original text continues,

"Picou tells me he saw the werewolf only this day se'nnight [evening]. He was down by the edge of his buckwheat field, and the sun had set, and he was thinking of coming home, when he heard a rustle on the far side of the hedge. He looked over, and there stood the wolf as big as a calf against the horizon, its tongue out, and its eyes glaring like marsh-fires. Mon Dieu! Catch me going over the marais tonight. Why, what could two men do if they were attacked by that wolf fiend?"

No willing villager could be found to escort Baring-Gould across the flats, and so he made his return trip alone. He did not encounter any *loups-garoux* that evening, but this was only the beginning of his relationship with the creature.

It may be assumed that the villagers were referring to a very large wolf, not a supernatural being, and Baring-Gould makes this admission toward the end of his encounter. Yet the mortal terror displayed by the villagers would light a spark in him, and he later wrote *The Book of Werewolves*, a collection of folk tales from around the globe dealing with the issues of lycanthropy and upright canines. It is largely a compilation of anecdotes and much older stories but is a fascinating and important work which displays the breadth with which these creatures were thought of even less than two hundred years ago.

If Baring-Gould's experience sounds familiar, then you have probably seen the well-loved cult classic film *An American Werewolf in London*. The opening scene of this film closely mimics the setting of Baring-Gould's experience, with some variation, before the film's protagonist is attacked and transformed into the movie's titular monster. Whether the filmmakers were inspired by *The Book of Werewolves* is a fact I have yet to ascertain, but it seems a strangely specific coincidence if not.

The werewolf has been with us since well before 1865, as Baring-Gould's work illustrates. *The Book of Werewolves* is packed with the mythology of Scandinavian, Prussian, German, English, Indian, Native American, Austrian and Middle Eastern peoples. With some variation as warranted by context, all of it deals with, or is adjacent to, the topic of upright canines and lycanthropic transformations.

But for all his research, the stories recorded by Baring-Gould are not the first to mention the werewolf in our history. In fact, some of the oldest known mythology on planet Earth mentions, or at least alludes to, the existence of upright canines.

Ancient Mesopotamia and Tiamat's Wolfmen

Scholars often refer to ancient Mesopotamia as the Cradle of Civilization. The earliest forms of government and religion sprung from here, propelling humanity along a trajectory that would, in many ways, ultimately place us where we are today as a species.

But it was also the birthplace of some of our favorite monsters. A panoply of bizarre creatures is to be found in ancient Mesopotamian writings and artwork. Some of archetypes we are most familiar with today, such as dragons and merfolk, are mentioned at this earliest place in known history. Countless cults and religions sprung up around belief in these otherworldly beings, such as Tiamat and her legion of unnatural monsters.

Among these was one which may be the forebear of the thing we call Dogman.

Tiamat is considered an elder god in the Mesopotamian pantheon. Much like Kronos of Greece, Tiamat was a malevolent being who was ultimately overthrown by the lesser god, Marduk, giving birth to a new age in which humanity might prosper. In her climactic battle with Marduk, Tiamat created an army of chimeric beings, which Marduk slew before dealing the final blow to Tiamat herself. *Enuma Elish*, also known as the Babylonian Epic of Creation, is the record from which these stories are drawn.

Among Tiamat's fighters was Urudimmu. The Gruesome Hound. The Mad Canine.

Urudimmu (or sometimes Uridimmu) was a fearsome being. As with most ancient folklore, there are varying depictions and interpretations of the creature. It has sometimes been interpreted as a human/lion hybrid, not decidedly canine, but recent work by modern scholars of the period suggests that the anatomy of the creature as crafted by Mesopotamian artisans may have been intended to depict a canine creature, not a feline one.

Interestingly enough, Urudimmu is not the only canine/human hybrid to haunt our Mesopotamian forebears. Another savage creature, this one far more infamous in the modern era, may be another ancestor of the creature we presently pursue.

The dreaded demon Pazuzu.

Many of us know Pazuzu today as the antagonist of the 1973 film *The Exorcist* (which I am still, at 35 years of age, too scared to watch). In his earliest forms, Pazuzu was not a demonic servant of Satan intent on tormenting the souls of American children. Like his cousin Urudimmu, he can be found in varying forms with contrasting natures and was depicted as both an antagonistic monster and a protective god-like spirit.

The appearances of both beings, especially interesting for the purposes of our study, is that of upright-walking humanoid canines. Pazuzu is often also seen with wings, a scorpion's tail, and other ghastly half-beast features. Ancient Mesopotamia seems to have been overwhelmed with human-animal hybrids, and we might spend pages exploring the lore of these and others - Lamashtu, Apkallu and Kusarikku represent humans mixed with lions, birds and bulls, respectively. Pazuzu and Urudimmu were likely based upon Akkadian Kalbu and Mastiff dogs, as both breeds are found throughout Babylonian art and were known to be present at this point in history.

These creatures are also preserved, at least by name, in the stories we tell in the modern day. Urudimmu is the name of a guardian monster in the seminal role-playing game Dungeons and Dragons, and as mentioned, Pazuzu has left an indelible mark on Hollywood.

The origin of the werewolf is difficult to trace, as it can be found in ancient Greece, Mesoamerica and Europe. Whether the hybrids of Mesopotamia represent their earliest incarnation is a question left to better minds than my own, but we can, at the very least, establish that these beings find at least some of their roots in the Fertile Crescent: The Cradle of Civilization.

The Jaguar Men of Mesoamerica

Greatly removed from the Land Between the Lakes, but quite a bit closer than Mesopotamia or Europe, we now find ourselves on the North American continent - hundreds of years in the past and a few hundred miles south, in the area today known as modern-day Mexico. Here we find a Latin American legend nearly in sync with any study of shapeshifters or werewolves - The Nagual.

At first glance, the Nagual may not be considered to this discussion, but I would argue that the inverse may be true. This supernatural entity of Mesoamerican tradition has a veritable wealth in common with both the werewolf of Europe and the Skinwalker of North America. Perhaps no great surprise, as the Inca, Aztec and Mayan peoples who recorded stories of the Nagual lived adjacent to the Native American lands where stories of the Skinwalker can be found to this day. A coincidence, perhaps, but coincidence seems to be a recurring trend in the study of the werewolf.

The Nagual - also referred to as Nahual or Nahuali - were important figures in ancient Mesoamerican cultures. In some incarnations they were considered spiritual leaders, shaman or healers, acolytes of the gods who would read the signs of nature and pass down messages from on high. In other societies they were an elite class of warriors, believed to be endowed with one key supernatural ability - shapeshifting.

According to a research paper titled *Nagualism: A Study in Native American Folk-Lore and History* by Daniel G. Brinton, Nagual sorcerers were purported to possess the ability to take on a variety of animal forms. Included were snakes, dogs, centipedes, weasels, owls, bulls and even animate balls of fire. Chief among their shifted forms, however, seems to be that of a jaguar, hence the common English name "The Jaguar Men."

Brinton's research paper was published in *Proceedings of the American Philosophical Society* in 1894, but his references are much older - he cites documentation of a Nagual ritual in Honduras circa the year 1530 as the earliest he was able to uncover.

Like our friend the Dogman, The Nagual are not content with being relegated only to the ancient past. Sightings of the Nagual persist in the modern day, with one occurring in the Mexican city of Veracruz in 2020. The creature was chased by villagers into a tree before allegedly changing shape and flying away, creating a panic and prompting coverage by local news stations. Let this serve as another example of a society in which shapeshifting beasts, or humans endowed with animalistic abilities, are still very much believed in.

The Month of the Wolf Men

The ancient Persian calendar, which divided the year into twelve months not unlike the one we use today, designated the eighth month between what we now consider October and November. Its name was *Varkazana* - Month of the Wolf Men, according to some translations. If we need any further proof that the relationship between wolves and humans was on the collective mind of our ancient ancestors, let this serve as a place to hang the proverbial hat. I was somewhat elated to make this discovery - my own son was born smack dab in the middle of *Varkazana,* while I was in the midst of completing the final draft of *The Texas Dogman Triangle.*

We might make a comparison to the prevalence of the flood myths in ancient mythology. While most are familiar with the story of Noah's Ark, the narrative of a global flood is found in religious and mythological texts from around the globe. A prominent example is *The Epic of Gilgamesh*, but deluge myths are also found in Africa, Asia, The Americas and even Oceania. Might the werewolf be something similar - an ingrained piece of mythology that, for one reason or another, nearly all our ancestors seemed to have in common?

A Modern Legacy

While the werewolf is an ancient creature, its claws are firmly set in the modern day. The

Nagual, European werewolves and even the dog demons of Mesopotamia provide something of a roster of counterparts to the Dogman of North America if we are inclined towards spectral or spiritual theories. After continued research into this topic and conversations with a growing list of witnesses, it has become difficult not to find myself on this precise line of thinking.

But more on that later.

Moving Forward

We have spent considerable time exploring the history and strangeness of The Land Between the Lakes. We have also examined the pedigree and nature of Dogman, in so much that we are able with brevity, and it is my hope that the preceding chapters will provide an image of what exactly (or, perhaps not exactly) my trip to the LBL was intended to focus on. The five chapters previous were also written, with minor adjustments and Chapter 2 notwithstanding, before I crossed the borders of Tennessee and Kentucky.

The following chapters will detail a series of encounters relevant to this discussion. There are many more, and this volume will not provide a comprehensive list. In the next chapter, I will happily explain why.

6
The Campsite - 1993

If the Dogman phenomenon is a legitimate event (and this volume is drafted on the notion that it is) then there can be little doubt that it has a presence in the Land Between the Lakes. An obvious element of this type of research is to review, outline, and examine as many documented encounters as can be done prudently. This was the first roadblock I encountered, having no area contacts or connections to the LBL outside of a few colleagues in the field who had spent time there (at least, that was what I thought). To chase every anecdote or mention of the LBL Dogmen I could find quickly proved an overwhelming task, and initially, I assumed it was impossible. At first draft I sought to compile a comprehensive list and timeline of Dogman encounters in and around the park, at least based on any information I could personally obtain, much as I had done during my research into the Texas Dogman Triangle.

This soon proved redundant, however, as retired law enforcement officer Martin Groves has already done that. There are a few names in 2023 which will inevitably, as the rain comes with the clouds, arise when one begins to research upright canids in general. With a focus on the LBL, some of those names become inescapable.

Martin Groves is one of them.

Martin has written two books on the Beast of the Land Between the Lakes - *Beasts Between the Rivers*, and *A Trace of Death: Beasts Between the Rivers*. One may note the usage of the older name for what is now called the Land Between the Lakes. Martin's books provide what is almost certainly the most comprehensive overview of the Dogman phenomena in this area currently available, and while this work endeavors to provide something similar, it lacks the detail and enumeration which Martin has inserted into his own books. As mentioned, Martin is a retired law enforcement officer, and after an encounter of his own opened his eyes to the reality of these creatures' existence, he began to meticulously record eyewitness reports as they arrived on his desk. In Martin's words, he began secretly investigating Dogman activity in the LBL in 1993, keeping a file of notes which recorded in detail dates, descriptions and, in some cases, fatalities. Encounters with the Dogmen of the Lakes are not limited to one infamous urban legend and a few questionable encounters online, as Martin's books (and the testimonies of other contemporary witnesses) well illustrate. I first met Martin at Small Town Monsters Monster Fest in June of

2023. We had little time to talk aside from passing introductions, but I found him to be warm, kind and altogether entirely likable. This is a common impression, and, in the scope of my research, Martin is universally liked and spoken well of by those in the community. In a niche where divisions and interpersonal politics can act as the number one obstacle to the collection and sharing of information, this is no small feat.

It was in November of that same year that we were able to engage in a one-on-one conversation, during the filming of *Dogman Territory: Werewolves of the Land Between the Lakes*. As noted, this trip was intended to serve the dual purposes of book-writing-research-trip and documentary-film-shoot, and Martin was at the top of my interview list. A sudden onset of allergies prompted my eyes to water impressively during the entirety of our talk, but fortunately the camera was not aimed at my face.

Martin speaks with the warm and reassuring baritone of a preacher presiding over Thanksgiving dinner. He smiles often, greets enthusiastically, and never hesitates to offer a compliment or affirmation. He has a beard that would put the heartiest lumberjack to shame, and one might be grateful that they were not a criminal operating in Martin's jurisdiction during his law enforcement tenure. He seems the type of man who might have ripped a tree stump out of the ground for fun in his younger days, and he carries himself with the slow confidence of a man who knows exactly what his hands are capable of. In a previous life I spent a decade and a half as an avid martial artist, and Martin has the distinct air of a guy who could, without too much effort, beat me up. With a little training, you learn to recognize that trait in the way a person moves.

Despite this, he seems the furthest thing from a violent person one could imagine and might seem more at home snapping pictures with young children dressed as Santa Claus than arresting murderers and chasing down felons in the lawless forested areas of Tennessee and Kentucky. And yet, that is how Martin spent his career.

As we've heard, Martin would begin to quietly and diligently collect and catalog information regarding encounters with upright canines in the 1990s. His notes are a treasure trove of data, the type of reference material that researchers would hike the Himalayas for, and a quick perusal of his books presents one with a reality that is difficult to deny, and even more difficult to accept.

But it was much more than a secondhand account which led Martin to track and record this information in the first place. It was his own experience which caught him in the gravity of the Dogman phenomenon.

Martin Groves

"I believe there is something in that park, animal or beast, that poses a threat to the general public."

Martin was camping in the Land Between the Lakes in 1993 in pursuit of a sabbatical from his innately stressful career. He was turkey hunting with a colleague, in an area adjacent to the Mount Pleasant Cemetery. This was a familiar activity - a born and bred outdoorsman, Martin's competence in the wilds was never in question, and there was no reason for him to assume that this particular trip would be anything but idyllic.

Martin and his companion encountered a third hunter during their trip. The man was bow hunting in the same area, and they met in a parking area on the outskirts of the hunting grounds. They shared a friendly dialog before going their separate ways. Martin believes this is one of the last conversations the man had while he was still alive.

During their first night at camp, Martin and his fellow hunter encountered no odd occurrences. On the following day, they parted ways and set out on separate hikes.

"I had a feeling I was being followed inside the woods. Behind me I could hear movement. I could hear a presence that I did not know if it was animal or if it was man."

The movement was close.

"200-300 yards, on the trail behind me, I could see movement in the woods."

Martin kept his eyes on the trees, and after a time, was able to discern a few outlines in the rustling brush.

"I could see there was two, possibly three animals that were tailing me."

The park is full of animals - he likely assumed that these were one of the many species known to reside there.

As he moved through the woods, he noted something large disturbing the nearby brush, closer than the apparent animals he'd noted before. At first, he assumed it to be another hunter, and called a greeting into the darkness. He received no reply.

He continued his trek and noted that whatever had failed to return his greeting was keeping step with him. When he moved, it moved. As he got closer to his camp, he began to hear sounds from the darkness.

"I could hear a distinct knock in the woods. It would be a large *boom* like the sound of an ax hitting wood."

As he approached his camp, he finally caught sight of whatever had been stalking him. He describes a humanoid form with a ragged outline - what he thought to be a man in a ghillie suit.

Still drawing closer to the camp, he began to hear whistling.

"Human like. A shrill whistle."

He assumed the noises to be from his camping partner, perhaps trying to get his attention. He'd been in the woods for hours. Perhaps his partner was concerned for his safety.

Upon returning to camp, he found his friend shaken. He'd known the man for years and immediately knew that something was wrong. He apologized for being so late in returning, but the man said that his distress came not from Martin's prolonged absence, but rather from the sound of something moving around the camp. He also described the sounds Martin had just heard - whistling noises, and booming knocks and bangs.

It was now fully dark.

"When it gets dark in the Land Between the Lakes... it gets dark."

This is a verifiable fact. In my own travels I have seldom, if ever, been to a place that is so completely dark after sunset. I can only compare it to my high school-era visit to the caverns of

Raccoon Mountain, a little over 200 miles south of the Land Between the Lakes near Chattanooga, TN. After proceeding to a depth of God knows how far underground, our guide instructed our group to stand very still and turn off our flashlights. Twenty years later, standing on the spot where his sighting occurred, Martin would make the same request of the film crew and myself. In both cases the effect was terrifying.

Martin describes it well when he says,

"It is as if you were in the seventeen or eighteen hundreds."

The campfire and a small kerosene lamp served as the only light sources, providing visibility for roughly fifteen to twenty feet. Enough to see some detail in the surrounding brush, but not nearly enough to create even the illusion of safety.

"I noticed what looked like a man standing behind a tree," Martin explains. A discussion was had over whether to break camp and take flight, but these are not the sort of men to be easily intimidated. The notion was, at least for the moment, discarded.

"At that point we were locked in. We were not going to be made to move by anything or anybody. This was our camp."

Then came the missiles. A section of tree was thrown from a cliff overlooking the camp site.

Then a larger one from the right. The men conferred, briefly, before readying their weapons.

"You have to imagine the darkness."

Martin re-emphasizes the pitch-black night beyond the perimeter of their meager light sources.

From the darkness came a bestial growl.

"I've been around bears; I've been around pigs - charging boars. I've been around all different types of animals. This was a growl like I have never heard."

Then came the fear.

"It was as if I was a child and I was five years old. Scared of a monster in the dark."

At this point, he was able to catch a look at his tormentor.

"I could see what I knew was not a man. I knew it was not an animal I had ever seen. And it was coming towards me. In the glow of the campfire and the glow of my kerosene lamp, I caught what I felt was an upright walking... it was not a bear. It was like a wolf. It was large, huge, it was still walking towards me. I discharged my weapon in its direction two times."

Firing a gun at nighttime produces a muzzle flare equivalent to the flash of a camera, Martin explains. The image produced by that flash is forever burnt in Martin's mind.

"It was intelligent. It knew that that firearm was dangerous to it because it moved. It went backwards before I fired on it."

This is an interesting detail. If the creature did in fact recoil at the sight of a firearm, it demonstrates a level of intellectualism far beyond that of most animals. The ability to recognize Martin's gun - an unnatural variable, not produced by the environment - as a potential threat indicates, at the very least, previous encounters with armed humans.

After the shot was fired, the creature fled. But it didn't turn tail and scamper back into the brush.

"It could jump and leap beyond any human understanding. It jumped to the rock face that was beside it, and in an instant, it was gone. It disappeared and went over the ridge beside us."

Martin fired again, accompanied by his friend. Martin found himself screaming to the backdrop of gunfire shouting orders to return to the truck. Martin jumped in the back of the pickup truck while his friend took to the driver's seat and started the engine. It was then that he looked back, weapon trained on the campsite that was now behind him.

There were two of them. Two towering canine forms, setting upon the campsite with long arms and sharp claws. Tearing up the tents, scattering supplies and gear.

If the creatures' goal had been to scare the hunters away, they had more than succeeded. But there would be more strangeness before the evening's end, and this portion of the encounter would further challenge Martin to reassess his view of reality.

While the wolf-like creatures ravaged the campsite behind the truck, another pair of bipedal forms emerged from the woods in front of it. Martin now saw what he believed to be the thing he had - mistakenly - identified as a man in a ghillie suit a short time earlier. One stood taller than the other. What their role in the chaos must have been is anyone's guess, and the hunters did not stay behind to investigate. Martin's friend hit the gas, and they took off in the pickup truck, at least as quickly as the terrain would allow. He describes the beings in terms that will paint a familiar picture to most reading this volume - Sasquatch. He makes particular note that these were not the friendly, doe eyed, loveable apelike creatures of pop culture, but had hideous, not quite human, not quite animal faces which were difficult to behold.

After their escape, Martin and his friend agreed to keep the incident to themselves.

"There is an unwritten rule that you will not talk of anything coming out of the park."

Law enforcement officers have pensions, families, reputations to consider. It was for this reason that Martin waited until retirement to come forward. Even his wife, who immediately noticed a change in Martin's demeanor, would not hear the whole story until decades later.

In fact, Martin's story was first shared publicly in the Small Town Monsters film *American Werewolves* after researcher Heather Moser was able to arrange an interview with him. It was after this that his books were published, drawn from the notes collected over three decades in the field.

There is a final detail to this story. It was later, upon exiting the park in the wake of his frightening encounter, that Martin would learn that the bow hunter he and his friend had encountered had been found dead.

The cause of death was determined to be an animal attack.

This would not be the last time Martin would cross paths with the Dogmen of the Lakes, nor would it be the only strange incident to occur in this area. We will return to both Martin's testimony and his campsite in short order.

7
Rumors - 1989

"You don't have to go very far. If someone talks to you and opens up, they've got a story," Mike says as we sit by the shore of Lake Barkley. The sun is out, and it's hotter than expected. The flies and ladybugs are out in force, but the discomfort is a low price of admission for what would soon prove to be a fascinating interview.

Mike Smith is a teacher, but he's held a variety of occupations in his time, including a stint working for the Fisher-Price toy company. He's lived near the Land Between the Lakes area for most of his life and regularly participates in cemetery cleanups with the non-profit group Between the Rivers. He has lived or worked in nearly every county which borders the park and is well versed in the culture and lifestyle of the region. He describes farming and fishing and factory workers. Close knit families and an industrious populace. In addition, "Moonshining was the thing with the LBL."

He is careful to state, however, that despite his diverse professional background, he has never undertaken that particular pursuit.

"Some of the first stories I heard about the Dogman were actually from the kids," he says, including stories that he heard while in high school. Teenagers have a unique swiftness with which they can spread information, and I was interested to learn that Dogmen occupied a portion of the high school gossip of Mike's youth.

Some of the stories he heard were aggressive encounters, further adding fuel to the idea of a dangerous creature and validating the rumor that residents have been seeing strange things in the area since well before the era of the internet. Stories spread through word of mouth, before the age of comment threads or cellular communication.

"This was before social media."

He would have his own encounter, if only second hand, that would help to cement his fascination with the strange goings on of the Tennessee/Kentucky border. It would be only the beginning of Mike's own strange journey.

He speaks of a restaurant he worked at in high school, and visiting the north end of Lake Barkley - the same lake we now overlook - after hours with friends who worked on staff.

"If you've worked in a restaurant, you know, people will get together after hours and hang out."

A few of Mike's friends had selected a particularly beautiful campsite, an apparent local favorite, and gone out to the site early to drop off firewood and other supplies.

"They heard something. It was growling and shrieking and yelling, coming through the brush at them."

The sound was of a large animal, but it was concealed by the heavy vegetation.

"They called it a Wampus Cat."

We met the Wampus Cat earlier in this volume (Chapter 3). Elijah Henderson would mention the creature as well in a separate interview, and it occurs upon reflection that perhaps the Wampus Cat is worthy of its own study.

The group quickly abandoned their evening plans, fleeing from the campsite without bothering to collect their belongings. After a frantic flight out of the park and a reunion with the rest of the group, Mike was selected to venture out later in the evening, asked by his fellows to retrieve the wayward camping supplies with one other man from the group. How Mike drew this especially short straw is unclear, but one must admire his tenacity. Having spent his life near and within the Land Between the Lakes, he attributed the sounds his friends heard to any number of known species, perhaps assuming their fright to be an instance of group hysteria. Teenagers are good at that, after all.

Upon returning to the site, Mike heard the noise himself. Whatever had scared the group away from Lake Barkley was still around. It was, as his friends described, very noisy and seemingly very large.

"It was hard to describe. I thought it was a mountain lion."

Mike thought perhaps what he heard may also have been a natural wolf and says that some red wolves are known to live within the park. He describes a whooping, snarling howl which rose in pitch as it crooned.

Mike made a speedy retreat. He did not revisit the site that night, or in fact, ever again.

Months later, reflecting on the event and discussing the strangeness of the night in question, one of Mike's friends would ask, "Do you know what happened over there?"

And that was the first time Mike heard the story of the massacre, in or around the year 1989. Mike has made frequent return trips into the park for leisure, many of them on foot and unaccompanied, but gives an exception to the lakeside retreat which played host to the frightening occurrence. He avoids the area now, seeking out other locations which are - perhaps - less inundated with potential Dogman or rogue Wampus Cats.

Putting it simply he explains, "There's a part I don't go to."

Inevitably, Mike has collected other stories of run-ins with the Dogmen of the Lakes. He relays another encounter of a young woman riding on horseback who became separated from her group near an area known as the Blue Hole. The location is a former iron refinement zone, and the decades of chemical and mineral reactions have given the mineral bed around the Blue Hole a distinct, eponymous color.

The Blue Hole sits near Laura Furnace, which was constructed in 1855 and was the last iron furnace to be installed in the Land Between the Rivers. Today the trademark blue rocks which litter the shore of the creek - a result of "slag" runoff - are protected artifacts and are illegal to remove. The Blue Hole is located off the 6th "wrangler" horseback trail within the LBL, along an almost twelve-mile stretch with various historical points of interest. In addition to the Furnace is the grave of the Little Drummer Boy. Nathan Futrell was only 7 years old when he served as the youngest drummer of the American Revolution. He would live to the age of 56 and pass away in 1829, despite the grave's deceptive nickname.

"It was my understanding that she was gonna take a different route with her horse. Sometimes if you want to run a horse, you know fair horses just stay in a line, so if you wanna do something extra with your horse you gotta get them away from the others. That was my understanding.

"She saw something, and it stood up, and she froze. It looked at her and walked the other way. She didn't go there again."

The presence of this location adjacent to an iron refinement area is an interesting footnote. One may notice as we proceed that iron is a recurring theme within this volume, for reasons we will explore later. Mike would have more stories to share and would document one with a striking piece of physical evidence, which we will examine after a short diversion.

8
The Thermal - 2022

Jessi and Joe Doyle are the minds behind the increasingly popular Hellbent Holler YouTube channel. They mix paranormal research with on the ground investigation, utilizing technical equipment, historical knowledge, and countless hours of combing through data for points of reference and factual foundations. They approach every case they investigate and every phenomenon that captures their interest with the healthiest type of skepticism imaginable - detailed, optimistic, and studious.

"We do field investigations. We don't collect a lot of stories; we don't take a lot of witness encounters." Jessi explains. As one would expect, plenty of witnesses do contact Jessi and Joe as a side effect of their public persona, but their primary focus lies elsewhere.

Jessi continues,

"Our main goal is to go out to these locations where people have had these experiences, and actually put boots on the ground, and get a lay of the land, and see what's actually going on. We hike into remote forests; take everything we have on our backs, and we film along the way."

Jessi has a strong background in the paranormal. "Paranormal" - used in the ghost/spirit/spooky sense - is a word which has become increasingly fluid in recent years but is generally still thought best applied to spiritual/supernatural phenomena. Joe, on the other hand, specializes in cryptozoology, and is accustomed to chasing after footprints and strange sounds in the woods at night.

"Jessi started off with more of a paranormal, ghost hunter type of background," Joe explains,

"I was more involved in physical bigfoot research. When we got together, we joined forces, and the whole goal of the project was to kind of advance these things beyond campfire stories. Collect any sort of data we could to back up what people were reporting seeing in the woods, haunted locations, things like that."

The marriage of their skill sets, literal and proverbial, and their unique approach to the topic of the unsolved, has provided something of a breath of fresh air to researchers like me. Those who seek to cut through the sensational world of outlandish claims and unsubstantiated rumors that permeate the world of the strange, as well as cliffhanger video endings that never go anywhere, and several of my other pet peeves, will find an oasis of entertaining and substantive content in the Hellbent library. Jessi and Joe provided not only essential research material to me as I wrote the *Texas Dogman Triangle*, connecting me with two witnesses whose stories had never been documented previously, but their work laid the foundation for much of my approach to this volume. I'm not alone in this - at time of writing, their YouTube channel is right on the cusp of fifteen-thousand subscribers.

Shannon asks the first in a series of important questions.

"What got you interested in Dogman?"

"Again, I was mostly focused on physical bigfoot type stuff," Joe says,

"I wasn't interested in ghosts, UFOs, definitely not in Dogman. At all. Matter of fact when the topic first came up it was pretty comical to us. We spent a lot of time making fun of the topic when we first started to hear about it."

It wasn't long however before second and third hand accounts began to slide into Jessi and Joe's DMs, to use a phrase I've heard is popular.

"We had a bigfoot researcher that I knew online, contact us going 'Hey man I've got a case that happened in your all's area, I don't know if you're interested in it but let me pass it along to you.' His daughter had seen an upright wolf on Christmas day, in an area about an hour and a half north of us."

They found the report interesting but chose not to pursue it any further. After all, and reports aside, werewolves were still a thing relegated solely to fiction. At least at the time.

"And then it was like the floodgates were opened." Joe says.

Reports began to roll in by the dozen, all concentrated north of Jessi and Joe's usual Appalachian stomping grounds. I had to clarify and asked how many reports they ended up dealing with in total.

"Over a hundred."

The nature of the descriptions themselves strikes a particular tone. Joe elaborates, "It was just odd the amount of reports we were getting for something we weren't associated with. The Dogman reports. We probably had about twenty or so of those, all in a little strip. It started in Rolling Rock, North Carolina going down to the southeast, with person after person reporting the same thing. Nobody was using the term Dogman. Everybody's calling them werewolves."

Jessi continues, "For the layman, the normal person who has these experiences, the closest approximation they have is 'werewolf.'"

Usually, the team takes the hottest month of the summer off, given the uncomfortable weather, leaving the woods to themselves for a short time.

This year was different. The continuing deluge of reports demanded investigation.

This was Dogman Summer; the nickname Jessi and Joe came up with for their skeptical expedition. The team canceled their usual sabbatical in favor of a dedicated period of additional research, braving the summer heat in search of werewolves. It was a lighthearted endeavor, and they expected nothing significant to come as a result.

But as we've said - this was Dogman Summer, and their expectations would soon be subverted.

They compiled a list of apparently active locations, mapped out a road trip, and loaded their impressive array of investigative gear into the Chevy Blazer ZR2. The 2004 sport utility vehicle had been restored by Jessi herself. Before long they were en route.

"The first one was the Land Between the Lakes" Jessi explains, "It was still kind of a lark for us. It was still kind of 'alright, let's go check this out' - because you hear about all of these stories, and all of this lore, and all of these rumors about what goes on in the Land Between the Lakes. And, other locations, but primarily you hear about the Land Between the Lakes."

"At what point did you realize that there's actually something there?" Shannon asks, regarding the whimsical nature with which Dogman Summer was conceived.

Jessi and Joe both seem to shift in their seats. The conversation takes a slight shift in tone. The Hellbent team's investigation would do the same.

"It was right before midsummer's night, and it's extremely hot," Joe says, "We're moving around on foot, on some hiking trails around where the '82 massacre is supposed to have taken place. The forest just goes dead quiet on us." He continues,

"And we start hearing something busting through the brush, to our left at that point. Our usual MO is whenever something like that happens, one of us focuses on it and the other one starts checking the backs and the sides."

"Because we don't know," Jessi adds, "whatever these things are, are they organized to a degree that they're using diversion tactics?"

Joe agrees and says, "The forest goes dead quiet. We had used the trip to the LBL as an excuse to buy a new thermal imager. And when I say we just got it, it literally showed up the day before we left. We were actually making arrangements for someone to pick it up off our porch if we left before it got there."

Jessi focuses her attention on the movement in the underbrush, while Joe employs the brand new thermal to survey the perimeter.

"Jessi's focused on whatever is busting through the brush, I'm scanning with this new thermal imager, and I scan from right to left, and I pick up an extremely strong heat signature. Pop back and I look at it and I'm not sure what I'm looking at, so I snap a photo of it. And it moves a little bit, it kind of shifts, and I'm like 'alright, whatever I'm looking at is aware that I'm here.' I had a flashlight hanging from a lanyard on my left wrist and I kind of fumbled with it."

Joe manages to catch a second photo before the creature disappears from view.

At this point the team was certain of one thing; there was something large in the brush. In addition, it seemed to be at least aware of their presence, perhaps even aware that it had been spotted. They made the decision to proceed to higher ground and advanced along the path, moving away from the gulley to a wider section of the trail.

Thermal imagers have very small screens. In order to review the two photos Joe had captured, they hooked the device up to a laptop and downloaded the files.

"It's something that's about six, six-and-a-half feet tall, and it's got extremely oversized pointed ears on the top of its head. What I saw didn't scream canine to me when I first saw it. If you had to ask me what it was, it would have looked like a giant bat. Muzzle, elongated, pointed ears."

The image seemed to defy explanation. Joe explains, "We reached out to a friend of ours who does a lot of predator hunting."

This friend was proficient in the use of thermal scopes for tracking and identifying wildlife, including large game. He stated in no uncertain terms that the image was not of a bear, coyote, boar, deer, or any other animal he could identify. What he did say however was, "It's alive - it's extremely hot."

"He had the thermal scope set to black hot," Jessi explains, "and it's the summer. You don't have a huge difference in the environment during the summer. Now in the winter the thermals are amazing, because there's such a contrast between living things and the environment around you. There were similar temperatures there, and this thing stood out. Whatever this was was giving off tons of heat."

The creature captured in the underbrush by Joe's thermal imager. Photo used with permission.

I asked the team to clarify what "black hot" means, not being well versed in cryptid-hunting field gear beyond your standard flashlight.

"It means that the hotter something is the darker it'll appear," Joe explains, "a thermal imager will basically look for differences in the temperature of the environment - so Jessi mentioned in the summertime it's not as effective because everything's extremely hot. There's not a big difference in your body temperature and the surrounding environment. Wintertime it just pops. When we were looking at deer earlier, we couldn't see them that well until they were highlighted against the sky... against the top of a hill."

This is important. As one can see, the shape captured by the thermal imager is jet black, clearly visible against the surrounding brush. Joe's hunter friend would remark, "It's hotter than a coyote would be."

Shannon then asks if this incident prompted the team to want a second thermal imager.

"Yes, it did," they say almost in unison, and Joe adds, "So, we got another one."

Jessi and Joe reached out to other researchers who were more seasoned in the Dogman phenomenon. In response, they received a bevy of eyewitness sketches purported to be the result of Dogman encounters. The most defining and consistent feature, and the one which they would immediately recognize, were the elongated, pointed ears.

"I can't say that we saw a Dogman, because I didn't see it with my naked eye," Joe explains,

"But we saw something that was *alive*, was six to six-and-a-half feet tall, had a muzzle, and has these extremely exaggerated, pointed ears on top. That - when I figured out I was looking at it- disappeared. We went back the next day and found a gully next to the path."

Jessi says, "We found the exact spot we were standing, and there's a ravine in the woods. So, whatever this thing was went down in the ravine. Joe's about six-three, so he went and got in the ravine and was looking over the edge exactly where this thing was, and you could tell actually on the ground there that the ground had been moved. There was moss on the ground that had been scraped and moved around, so something *was* there. But he got into that ravine, and looked over, and you saw just about the amount of whatever this thing was looking over on him (Joe). It's about his height, whatever this thing was, but much larger on top. The head was much larger."

"That was kind of shocking." Joe adds before saying, "Later when we met Martin Groves and had the opportunity to show him the image - he just flipped out. Because he said the ears were exactly what he'd encountered back in '93 at that point. And that kind of took any uncertainty away from me. It's a hard thing to swallow. We even looked at, 'what other animals have large pointy ears?' I've gone as far as to see if there had been like a kangaroo that escaped from a local zoo."

No such records, indicating any escaped animals, have been found.

The creature seemed to move when Joe fumbled for his flashlight. His assumption is that this action gave away that he had noticed the thing, whatever it was, and it was immediately after that it fled into the ravine.

"A lot of these ravines - they don't have leaves or anything in the bottom of them. They do this time of year, but not in the middle of the summer," Jessi says. It's not difficult to imagine someone, or something, skulking in the shadows of the gulley to gain a stealthy view of the trail.

"It's almost like a superhighway that goes all over the peninsula. Some of them are seven feet deep. If you're looking directly across, you can't tell it's there."

Jessi is right. I would soon find myself standing in just such a creek - the very same one, in fact - barely able to see the trail I had just stepped off of.

Joe would lead me to the precise spot in November of 2023, just a few hours after this interview was conducted. I stood where the creature stood and leaned into the embankment as it seemed to have done. I was barely visible back on the trail, where the rest of the crew were assembled, filming a dialog piece between Shannon and Jessi. I felt, perhaps, that I was in the wrong place - I am frequently reminded by the crew to keep up and stay in the frame when we traipse through the wilderness, and have repeated this pattern on both major productions in which I've been involved - but had I not followed Joe off of the path, I would lack the perspective to make the following statement:

The creature that Jessi and Joe saw stood at least six feet tall. Anything smaller simply doesn't make sense. The size of the head and shoulders seems to preclude a smaller animal skittering up the embankment, and the rise is too tall for anything shorter to be seen.

"Was there any indication that there was more than one?" Shannon asks.

"We never saw what was making noise to the side of us. So that could have just been a deer, that could have been something else, we don't know." Joe says.

"But with the timing of having that thermal..." Shannon prompts.

Joe replies, "It's extremely odd. And I know I'm building a narrative here, I know that, but what it seemed to me is that whatever it was, it was observing us. No visible light, again, the thermal imager is passive. It doesn't even put out infrared light. It's just reading body heat. And it almost seemed that when I started focusing on it, it shifted a little bit"

As mentioned, Joe snapped two separate photos of the creature with the thermal imager. Between the photos, the figure changes position.

"You can see an eye in one of them, but you don't see it in the other one."

Both thermal captures. Hellbent Holler provides a detailed analysis and comparison in their series *The Werewolf Experiments.*

Shannon asks if this encounter has prompted the team to reassess any previous activity they've documented. After years spent researching the unsolved, had the evidence they'd captured reframed things they'd already drawn conclusions on?

"Very much so." Joe says.

Jessi continues, "As soon as this happened, we really had to kind of rethink a lot of stuff and really reflect on experiences that we had had. You start out and you do this for years and you're like 'okay, there's something going on in the woods, a rock was thrown, you hear this kind of noise in the woods.' And the first thing your brain goes to is Bigfoot. But the more that we've done this and gotten more information, and now this whole Dogman thing is thrown into the mix, now you have to kind of reassess - are those past experiences what I thought they were? Or is this new information... is this going to change everything? Do I need to reassess how I interpret what is going on in the woods?"

After the encounter, the Hellbent team thought it best to return to base for the night. Yet this odd crossing of paths, lasting only a few seconds, would send dramatic waves through the Dogman community as alleged proof of the Beast Between the Lakes. There is plenty of conjecture in comment threads as to what this image is actual proof of, but for my part, I've seen few pieces of evidence that are more, or even as, compelling.

This is not the only odd occurrence to beset the team during their dozens of hours in the LBL's range. They've also witnessed strange lights, which we might compare to orbs, moving around and above the wood line. They've documented long gash marks on trees, which in my mind most immediately resemble photos of alleged Dogman claw marks captured in the Dallas, Texas area.

In an abandoned shack, they discovered a subterranean tunnel concealed by a trap door. The passage plunged seemingly infinitely into the darkness, and where it leads remains a mystery. Within the tunnel - which dropped several feet down from the ground level - were an assortment of bones, most of them unidentifiable, which had been broken by something of considerable strength. The marrow had been seemingly drained. We might assume this to be the work of a known predator, but one may be interested to learn that the door to the shack was closed and latched. This material is covered extensively on the Hellbent Holler YouTube channel.

We discuss additional matters before we conclude, but the content of these conversations becomes relevant elsewhere in this volume.

At the end of this fascinating and somewhat frightening saga, Jessi explains, "We looked at each other, and we went - 'Crap. I guess Dogman's real. Guess we're doing Dogman now.'"

This prompts laughter all around, and Joe continues, "It's not really a topic that we set out to get involved in. Because you take the craziness that any of these fields have - UFOs, hauntings, bigfoot, there's always a certain amount of drama and craziness going on. There's ten times that in the Dogman community." Joe admits. At this point I catch myself nodding deeply, all too aware of the 'craziness' in question.

"If I had my druthers, I would much prefer to have had a Bigfoot thermal image that was really really good. That would have been great." Joe says.

Jessi agrees, "It would be less complicated at this point."

Addendum: The Kentucky Goblins

There is one other cryptid which came to my mind while reviewing the details of Jessi and Joe's encounter. I may be grasping at straws, but a particular story from the 1950s - only thirty-some-odd miles removed from the LBL and mentioned in Chapter 3 - bears at least one strong physical parallel to the figure silhouetted by the thermal image. UFO aficionados are aware of the Kelly/Hopkinsville encounter of 1955, in which a family spent hours engaged in actual combat with alleged extraterrestrial beings. UFO sightings lit up the sky, and before long, several small, garishly bizarre creatures began to make appearances on the Sutton family farm. They were short, less than four feet in height, and were seen to levitate and vanish into thin air. Their most striking physical feature, and the one most represented in artist interpretations, are oversized, pointed ears.

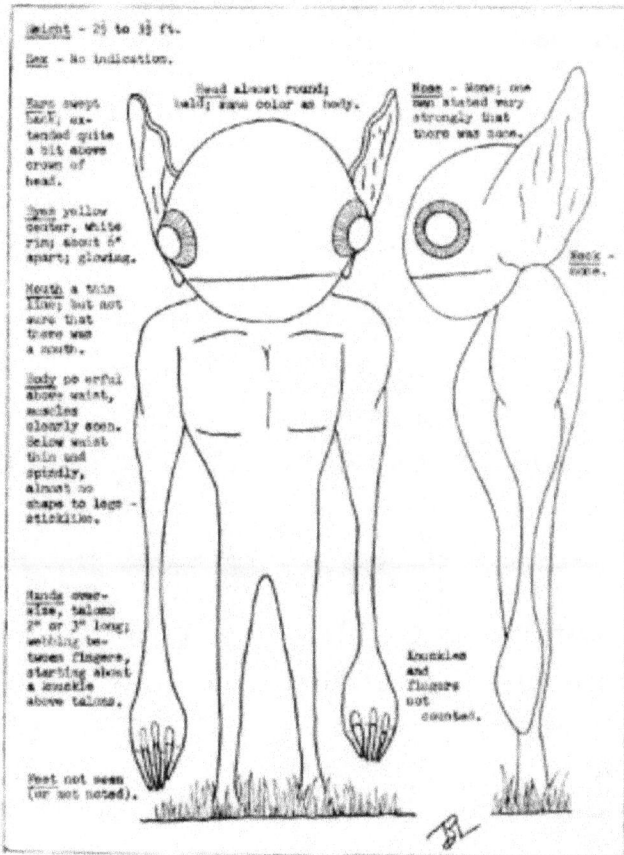

Another odd parallel which seems relevant is the purported resistance of the Kentucky Goblins to gunfire. Several were shot with both buckshot from a pump action shotgun and rounds from a .22 rifle during their multi-hour-long assault on the Sutton farmhouse. Damage from stray rounds littered the property, and yet not a single alien body was found. The creatures made metallic noises when shot, the sound likened unto an empty bucket. In nearly every Dogman encounter I can think of in which the creatures are subjected to gunfire, they seem to respond with near indifference. While Jessi and Joe did not take to shooting at whatever was seemingly stalking them, Martin Groves did. And as Joe mentioned only a short while ago, Martin would immediately describe the figure shown in the thermal image as familiar.

I will by no means die on the "the goblins were actually werewolves" hill, and in truth there is little other correlation between the ongoing Dogman phenomenon and the Sutton family's encounter in 1955. The goblins were, after all, described as being between three and four feet in height, and could apparently levitate and glow in the dark. Hardly a companion to the thing in the thermal photograph. However, the notion that the image captured by Hellbent Holler and eyewitness descriptions of the Goblins are at least somewhat similar was a difficult one to suppress, and as such, it is included here.

9
Travel Log #2: The Woods are Lovely, Dark and Deep

11/3/23
9:39 PM CST

The Bunkers

We drove via caravan from the northwest side of Lake Barkley into the LBL proper, leaving our base of operations at approximately five PM local time. I hopped in the back of Seth's Jeep Wrangler, which made quick work of the steep inclines of both the driveway of the rental house and the winding roads which lead into the recreational area. I had hoped to experience a bit of off-roading in the electric blue Breedlove Mobile, but the drive to our destination consisted of fairly well paved roads.

After a forty-five-minute jaunt we pulled up a narrow slope and parked along the edge of Mt. Pleasant Cemetery. We'd followed Jessi and Joe Doyle, the two-person investigative team known online as Hellbent Holler, in search of what many consider to be the place where four people lost their lives in the summer months of the early 1980s. The years Jessie and Joe have spent researching this place have proven invaluable thus far, and all that remains is to accompany them on a trek through the proverbial wolf's den.

We slowed and parked alongside Mt. Pleasant Cemetery. Progress by vehicle became impractical here, even with the Wrangler's off-road capabilities in our arsenal. It lacked the seatage to accommodate our entire group, and an up-close look was necessary for what would come next.

We proceeded on foot then, after taking a few minutes to situate equipment and personnel. Amongst our number was Aleksandar Petakov, outdoorsman and noted Sasquatch researcher, who kindly entrusted me with a monocular thermal scope. As the group proceeded, I began to fall behind, bewitched by the *Predator*-style view of the thick forest that the device provided.

We walked in a loose parade line as I eagerly listened to Joe describe he and Jessi's research into this area. We've entered what is commonly thought of as the massacre site, but Joe points out that it contains a few red flags when trying to designate it as a former campground. The road is narrow, and even accounting for years of growth, it's difficult to imagine full size recreational vehicles ever setting up shop here. The trail gives way to a slope on one side - a consistent feature in the Land Between the Lakes - which leads into a deep gully, the likes of which no RV has ever forded successfully.

After what must have been less than one hundred yards, flashlight beams were trained on a dilapidated cinder block structure to the right, which jutted out from the leaves and skeletal clusters of foliage. It was a short, squat, roughly ten-by-ten cube - one of the notorious "bunkers" said to be littered throughout the park. The Hellbent team explains that this may have been a rainwater cistern at one time, but that the exact nature of these structures remains unknown.

We proceeded farther down the hill, along what was at one time the route to an abandoned TVA work camp. Some remnants of the station remain, including another pair of bunkers. The first was without a proper entrance, due to erosion or construction or both, but the ceiling had caved in and was nearly level with the top of the rise into which it had been built. While the rest of the crew adjusted cameras and microphones, Shannon and Jessi shone flashlight beams into the pitch-black opening. I remember little of what was said here, enthralled to have finally reached this place, but do remember mumbling, "I'm gonna go in there."

Gloved hands pressed on porous, dilapidated concrete, and hiking shoes barely broken in scraped against the rusty rebar frame that fringed the opening. I dropped four, perhaps five feet to the ground below, crunching into a pile of leaves and decades-old garbage. It yielded little, save a feeling of gratitude at not being here alone; should something terrible happen, there were at least people around to pull me out. I fumbled with my phone and tried to get as many usable photos as possible, but my gloves and the dim transitional light made this an arduous undertaking. I dug around some in the trash with the toe of my shoe, finding a Pepsi can with a label that dated it to the 1960s.

The next bunker was easier to enter. It sat at ground level, and the entrance was unobstructed. The team shuffled inside, camera lights illuminating the spiders and crickets which adorned the graffiti-stained walls. It was then that Joe stomped twice in the center of the dirt packed floor and said, "You don't ever hear about this."

For instead of a dull, earthy thud, Joe's stomping boot yielded a hollow, humming bass note. I played drums with a focus on hand percussion for several years, and the sound reminded me of the goatskin djembe that I keep in my office.

The floor was hollow. A space of indeterminate size was beneath our feet. We speculated as to the material makeup of the floor, and in a moment, I was gouging away at the hard packed soil with a jagged junk of cinder block.

Four, five, six inches deep and I was still hitting dirt, but with each strike the metallic boom echoed beneath us. At last, I managed to scrape away an inch-long portion and expose the flooring it was hiding - metal. Hard, cold, ancient steel.

Still drying mud along the bunker's eastern wall led me to a rust-ringed, half buried drainpipe. With a precise angle from my flashlight, I was able to see some of the opening into which the pipe led, but the accumulated detritus and pressing urgency of our timetable prevented me from digging any further. Pictures sent to my wife when cell reception returned were responded to with, "Blair Witch vibes."

I could only agree.

We proceeded further down the hill, along a winding path in near pitch black. The sun still lingered when we arrived on the scene, but in the short time we'd been there night had fully descended. Jessie and Joe led the way while Aleks brought up the rear, the rest of our party interspersed between. We made cacophonous progress, crunching through the thick fallen leaves beneath our feet, ankle deep in the work of the autumn abscission. I was reminded by my companions, more than once, to keep pace with Shannon and the camera crew; the call of the thermal scope nagged at me and slowed my hike. In truth, I'd have liked to linger in the area for as long as possible, taking in the atmosphere and listening for bestial howls from the shadowed forest, but we had another place to visit before calling it a night.

One of the "bunkers" of the LBL. Photo by the author.

The Kill Site

Following the trail, we find ourselves in an area which is far more conducive to the details of the massacre story. A mile or more into the woods, past the remnants of a Tennessee Valley Authority work camp, we come to a stop on a pebbled beach at the edge of Lake Barkley. Despite our remote location, we cross paths with another researcher - a colleague of Aleksandar Petakov's, a member of the Bigfoot community.

We aren't the only ones in search of strangeness tonight. Motes of brown and light tan meet black water. The lake is still, and the night is quiet, save our own clomping progress through the leaves and twigs underfoot.

This may be the place where it happened. The place where four people are alleged to have died at the hands of an impossible horror, sometime near the beginning of the 1980s.

Coming here was inevitable, and I'll admit that I arrived with certain expectations. A sense of foreboding, ethereal vibes, the sense of being watched, perhaps. I've always had an odd reaction to crime scenes and cemeteries - my former career provided me ample encounters with the former, and my current one plenty of visits to the latter.

Here, though, that anticipated energy is not present. Perhaps it's the lights and cameras, the timetable which is slimmer than I'd like or the fact that I didn't come here alone.

After filming some B-roll and a few lines of dialogue, we hear a mechanical whir coming from the east. A helicopter soars overhead. We hear it before we see it, and Jessi catches it on the thermal scope, moving our way from the opposite bank.

"Got him," she says, and we all squint in the direction she gestures.

This is the fourth chopper we've seen during our short visit. The first appeared during the filming of the dialog scene this same morning, and the second and third flew in formation in the same area, later in the afternoon. One can't help but think of the rumors of government cover-ups, or the idea that we're being observed. Apparently, this is a normal occurrence in the park, but its placement alongside key investigative moments has been striking.

What did or did not happen in this space begins to seem inconsequential. If there was evidence to be found, save the remnants of outdoor showers and the remaining "bunkers" it would likely have been found a long time ago. No shortage of outdoor adventurers and cryptid hunters have scoured this place over the last four decades, nevermind the inevitable erosion brought on by the elements. I didn't come here expecting answers or evidence - in truth, I don't know what I expected - but I can say with relative confidence, having now stood on or near the infamous spot, that something akin to the "massacre" *could* take place in a location like this one. Everything fits - the woods, the near isolation, the darkness.

The darkness is pervading.

The location makes sense. It's scenic, and campers would awake to the sun glinting the lake's glassy water. It's isolated, at least a mile from any paved roads, and the only artificial light that we didn't bring with us comes from the cell phone tower, vertical red eyes blinking from beyond the distant ridge. It sits reasonably close to the remnants of a campground shower, and provides easy access to fishing, swimming and hiking. Forty years ago, with better-kept roads and some attention by the TVA, it might have been a prime campground.

It might have been many things.

Lake Barkley, KY, at the potential site of the "LBL Massacre." Taken after dark & brightened to show detail. Photo by the author.

10
Chasing the Massacre

Overview

We may argue that the fixation many of us share with the Dogman phenomenon relative to the Land Between the Lakes stems from one case. It concerns the deaths of four people which allegedly took place adjacent to the town of Grand Rivers, though its precise location remains a matter of debate. In truth, most of the details of this story have been subjected to so much revision, speculation, and circulation online in the last few years that any single aspect can be difficult to nail down with anything measuring certain accuracy. There is, however, a common narrative, and items which are consistently cited enough that we may consider them at least anecdotal data points of the case in question. I have done my best in this chapter to gather, examine, research, and summarize as many of those data points as I can. My success in this challenge is left to your interpretation.

Continuing an exploration of this narrative leads one down a variety of speculative corridors, some abstract, and some historical. The entire idea surrounding this case is one of abject horror, human mortality, and the ways in which folklore and conjecture intersect with real world history. We can guess, endlessly, what occurred in the Land Between the Lakes in the early 80s, or we can examine the available evidence - scant as it is - and arrive at conclusions more pragmatic than the standard internet "creepypasta" which has for so long permeated discussions surrounding the Beast of the Land Between the Lakes.

Or the Land Between the Rivers.

What Happened

The story is available in nearly every form online. Blog posts, YouTube videos, TikTok shorts, Facebook and Reddit discussion threads, podcasts, documentaries - including *Dogman Territory*, a film I was personally involved in - and even more minute formats such as memes and short-text graphics. Entire books have been dedicated to its study, including one by area local Steve Causey titled aptly *The LBL Massacre*, which was published in 2023. Even my colleagues at the North American Dogman Project have produced an hour-long documentary concerning the LBL and the story in question, simply titled *NADP - Land Between the Lakes Documentary*.

It is a ghastly, brutal tale which smacks of an internet "creepypasta," and I will not split hairs or deny the fact that when I first heard it, I dismissed it as pure fiction. In truth, after journeying to the LBL, visiting the alleged location of the event, speaking with multiple researchers and even an alleged witness, I am still on the proverbial fence as to just how much truth there is behind this event. It would seem difficult to deny that *something* happened, and it is often posited that even jokes and lies bear small seeds of truth. As a believer in many bizarre things, I am hesitant to write it off entirely, but my own opinions are likely of little interest to most who may be reading this. The reader is encouraged to take their own stance; we will examine this case from as many angles and with as much contributing information as we have been able to gather. I do not purport to be "in the know" or have discovered some secret the rest of the world is not privy to, but I have been fortunate enough to make the acquaintance of several researchers who have recently been involved in trying to shed more light on this case. And in one instance, a man who claims to have been there.

Those familiar will recognize this story as "The LBL Massacre," or a near variation thereof. It is also commonly referred to as the story of The Beast of the Land Between the Lakes.

Allegedly, two campers stumbled upon what at first appeared to be an abandoned campsite sometime in the spring or summer of 1983. The year of the event is one of many details which seems to be in question, as it has also been "traced" to the late 70s or perhaps earlier in the 80s. This, like many other variants within the saga, seems to depend upon who is telling the story.

The campsite which the hikers discovered was home to an RV in what is supposed to have been a popular campground. Further inquiries seem to indicate that the RV was a newer model, recently purchased, and contained the effects and a large sum of cash belonging to the victims.

A family of four - a father and mother, teenage son, and younger daughter, were found at the campsite. They had been brutally murdered, and it is purported that the scene was especially gruesome. The father and son were said to be lying in pools of their own blood outside the vehicle, while the mother was found inside. Words such as "mangled," "mutilated," and "mauled" have come up in countless interviews and discussions regarding the event, my own inquiries being no exception.

The hikers reported the incident, and a legion of government officials - state police, park police, local law enforcement, perhaps even federal officers - descended upon the scene shortly after the bodies were discovered.

The site was cleaned up, the bodies removed, the vehicle towed away, and the campground in question was closed. Obituaries fitting the description seem to be non-existent, and newspaper articles concerning the deaths of a family of four for this time frame are also suspiciously absent. It won't take long for those adjacent to the unsolved/paranormal communities to speculate that, if this event truly took place, a government cover-up is in play. Why else would there be no record of it, if it happened? Government cover-ups are another aspect of the LBL's strangeness, which is commonly speculated on, and even tacitly confirmed by the testimony of former law enforcement personnel (the statements made by Martin Groves in Chapter 6, for example).

Some details which seem oddly specific and yet are discussed and speculated over in countless tellings of this story, are that there may have been two of these creatures present at the attack, not just one. In addition, it is sometimes said that a member of the family was wearing cologne or perfume which emitted a scent pungent enough to draw the attention of the Dogman/men, precipitating the attack in the first place. One version I stumbled across conjectured that the beasts may have been drawn to the site because the mother of the family was in the midst of her monthly menstrual period. I'll break 'character' for a moment and state, in no uncertain terms, that this theory sounds, to me, incredibly stupid, and is couched in threads of sexism and medieval ignorance. I also ran it past several members of the veterinary community who seemed to share my opinion.

In some versions of the story, the body of the youngest family member, the daughter, is said to have been found in a tree near the motorhome. A favorite detail amongst tellers is that one of the responding officers walked underneath the tree, making a cursory inspection of the area, when a drop of blood fell onto his head or face from above, prompting him to train the beam of his flashlight upward, at which time he discovered the corpse of the youngest victim.

To call this an unpleasant tale might be an understatement, and the overt nature of the violence which would have taken place is one aspect that has prompted much skepticism from the research community. Cryptid encounters don't end with mutilated bodies and missing families; they end with blurry photos and sometimes being interviewed by a documentary film crew.

But then again, maybe that's too easy of an answer.

Rumors

The earliest documented incarnation of this story that can be traced is the 2007 documentary from Barton Nunnelly titled *Hunt the Dogman: High Strangeness in Kentucky*. The 25-minute film is a no frills look at the presence of the Dogman entity in the LBL, told in the form of an interview with one Jan Thompson.

If Thompson's intent in relaying the story and appearing in the documentary was to cash in or sell out, it seems an odd and poorly selected place to do so. As the earliest public witness to speak about the "LBL massacre," Thompson was bringing a little-known story into a public light - not attempting to latch on to an existing narrative. It is evident from watching *Hunt the Dogman* that there was no million-dollar payout for Thompson on the table when she agreed to the interview. Cryptid documentaries are notoriously made on minimal budgets, and in 2007 there were far fewer people interested in the subject matter. At the very least, the widespread acceptance we see today of the topic of cryptozoology was in a much earlier state.

The story is alleged to have also appeared online in a written form by Jan, and there are websites which still host what they purport to be the original testimony, but the story can be heard in Jan's own words in Barton Nunnelly's documentary. Jan would state that she first heard the story in or around the time that it happened, while she was working as a gas station attendant near the Land Between the Lakes. She claims that two law enforcement officers who responded to the scene relayed the details. Jan would also share an additional encounter she experienced early in her life, wherein a boy she knew was attacked by a similar creature while riding his bike through the woods.

In 2020, the Cryptid Studies Institute produced an hour-long documentary called *The Bloodthirsty Beast of LBL*, which is still available on YouTube. The team provided a comprehensive overview of the incident, even visiting an area they believed to be the site of the massacre. True to form for CSI, the video presents an objective and unbiased look at the story coupled with on the ground investigation and is a tremendous resource to those hoping to cut through the clickbait-y muck which has personified this tale.

A short time after their documentary aired on YouTube, Elijah and Johnny Henderson of the Cryptid Studies Institute would be contacted by a man calling himself Roger. Roger not only claimed to have additional information regarding the LBL massacre - he also claimed to be a survivor and witness of the event in question. This bombshell would immediately reverberate throughout the research community, and at time of writing is still hotly discussed. In a very short time, Roger's account has become an inseparable piece of the LBL Dogman puzzle.

The Survivor

In the follow-up video to their initial exploration of the LBL, Elijah and Johnny open by stating they may have gotten a few details wrong in their first video. They also state that they've been threatened with a variety of unseemly consequences should they continue to chase after the topic. Whether these threats are credible, or the work of a fringe wing of the cryptid community with nothing better to do is a matter I cannot deduce. Such lunacy certainly exists within the cryptozoology field; but the fact remains that the impact of the LBL massacre continues to ripple, inciting responses from a panel of interested parties.

Roger's testimony contained a breadth of additional details not found in popular narratives of the LBL massacre. The following quotes are taken from Elijah and Johnny's original interview, which was available on YouTube at time of writing.

When asked why he chose to come forward now, forty-odd years after the deaths took place, he says,

"It's time," stating that up until this interview he simply didn't want to talk about it.

Roger reiterates that the victims in this story were really people who lost their lives and speaks with an appropriate tone of reverence.

"This story shouldn't be glamorized in any way."

Roger claims that he met the family in question during Christmas vacation of 1981. His relatives owned land in LaGrange, Indiana, and while visiting he became acquainted with Levi, Dianne - who went by Lizzy - and their children Steven, age 13, and Connie, the younger sister, age 9. Roger states that Steven was "a couple years" younger than him, placing him in junior high at the time of the event. He describes a family dynamic which indicated obedient children, a kind and attentive mother and a protective, providing father.

Over time Roger formed a friendship with Steven and Connie, and in April of 1982 the siblings' parents acquired a brand-new motorhome which would serve as their primary residence. They had apparently at one time been a part of the Amish community in LaGrange but left for reasons which Roger declines to comment on. The family planned to leave the area and put the new motorhome through its paces on a cross-country trip, and Roger was invited to come along. The family's destination was a campground in the "Tennessee/Kentucky area" - the Land Between the Lakes. Roger even provides what he believes to be the make, model and year of the RV - a 1982 Holiday Imperial.

The travelers departed on April 7th, between nine and ten o'clock in the morning, and proceeded without incident along the approximate 450 miles between LaGrange and the Land Between the Lakes. He states that they arrived at the park near dusk, between five and six o'clock.

The drive from LaGrange to the LBL is approximately seven hours by car, so accounting for the occasional stop for food, fuel and human nature, the family's arrival time would seem to make sense.

He describes in detail the controls which would settle the motorhome in for the night, then explains that Levi and Steven walked off about a hundred feet or so to collect firewood. They would have little time to enjoy their selected campsite.

Roger was inside the RV with the doors closed, busying himself with mundane tasks, when he heard yelling, at which time he exited the motorhome and "came around front." It was here that he got his first look at a creature that would haunt him for decades thereafter.

"Steven was being attacked by this thing. Levi shot, and he hit Steven, and he hit this thing in the shoulder."

This is an interesting detail - were this a fictitious construction, the inclusion of a man accidentally shooting his own son is an odd bullet point in the narrative. He continues,

"And I wanna make a point that Levi did not kill his own son. He was already dead, I think, from this thing's attack. And after Levi shot, this thing came over, and got ahold of Levi, and I believe how this thing killed him was it either bit him or broke his neck. One or the other. I threw open the main entrance door, and I had that .410 shotgun, and when he [the creature] got back in sight as he passed the main door, I just, it all went black, but all I did was fire, and I hit it. And it did go down. And it got back up. And this is what they found in the tree. It was not Connie. I don't know where that awful tale come from, but they did not find her in the tree."

"It was the creature itself that they found in a tree?" Johnny asks.

"Absolutely."

This is a key deviation from the popular version, and an important thing of note when examining Dogman encounters. Typically, these beasts are regarded as being either immune or resistant to ballistic weaponry and is a defining aspect of many of the cases I have researched. The detail of the youngest family member being found in the tree permeates most versions of this story, but Roger's account places her in the motorhome.

Roger states that he became afraid at this point in the encounter. He dropped to the ground, rolled underneath the motorhome, and hoisted himself up into the framework. It was then that he heard screaming from inside the vehicle.

Somewhere in his mind Roger assumed that Connie and Dianne would be coming with him as he exited the motorhome, perhaps following him into the imagined safety of the undercarriage, but this was not the case.

"Whatever it was got a hold of them. I could hear it through the floorboard, through the bottom. It was muffled but I could hear it. And it, ah - oh Jesus. It was over fairly quick. After about, I suppose, time was flashing but I suppose it was 15 minutes, I rolled out and I ran that whole way, through the entrance [of the camping area]."

Roger flew as fast as his feet could carry him. After an indeterminate period of time - he estimates the duration to be fifteen minutes or so - he happened across a local driving a blue pickup truck. A dialog ensued, and Roger relayed what he had just witnessed. The man drove Roger to his own home, a local farm, and the man and his wife alerted the authorities while Roger attempted to recover.

In the approximate hour since the attack, Roger states that a bevy of official looking people had descended on the scene, including older looking military vehicles which he likened to World War II era equipment. The vehicles were unmarked, and no decals or logos representing any agencies were visible.

So, what, exactly, did Roger see? During their interview, Johnny asks him to describe the creatures. Without a description, we may be talking about any number of known or unknown animals. This could easily be the work of regular wolves, sasquatch, or human culprits.

Roger describes a build resembling an athletic man in a hairy suit, with defined musculature and distinctly canine facial features. The ears he describes as "more down," while the feet were apparently long and narrow.

Some purported Dogman "evidence" to be found online features photographs of footprints matching this description; we will examine one example in an upcoming chapter.

The creature's hands, or forepaws, were also visible. They were over-large, disproportionate to the rest of the body, and had visible claws which Roger states were, "A couple inches at most."

They stood at a height of just over six feet - "six-four, six-five" - an imposing figure, to be sure, but not the towering inhuman monstrosity of some encounters.

"I thought, I really thought, for years after to be honest, that these were people in suits robbing, or trying to murder us. That's what I had thought. And at that time, I knew nothing about Dogmen and still don't know a lot about them to be quite honest."

Roger also provides a detailed description of the motorhome's interior, giving a complete verbal tour beginning at the entrance. Johnny explains that he and Elijah looked up the model of motorhome that Roger claims to have ridden in, and that his description of the Imperial's interior is spot-on.

Roger alleges that the date was April 7th, 1982, and that the attack took place sometime between five and six o'clock. Weather records for the area concerning the date in question list the average temperature at around 60 degrees with possible rainfall throughout the day. Johnny also confirms Roger accurately describes the amount of light relative to the time of day as it would have been in the Land Between the Lakes at that time, but Roger admits his estimation of the time may be off.

"It was a long time ago and I'm trying to estimate the best I can."

Roger returned to Cedar Rapids, Iowa, where he remained at the time of the interview's recording. He didn't share the story throughout his life but did eventually relay it to his wife.

"I still didn't know what I had went through to be honest, or what these things were," he says near the end of the interview, "I still don't. If anyone asks me... were these walking, erect wolves? Werewolves, Dogmen? I wouldn't be able to answer truthfully. Because they looked so much, they stood so much like humans, the only thing that was, you know, different about them was the build, the hair, things like that."

2023

After listening to this interview, it became obvious that Johnny and Elijah had done a lot of my work for me. Specifically, investigating the model of RV and looking into family records in the LaGrange area. From here, there was only one thing to do - speak to Roger himself.

I emailed Roger in October of 2023 and was pleasantly surprised to receive a reply almost immediately. We had a brief preliminary conversation, and in November of 2023 I spoke with Roger and Shannon LeGro on a recorded call.

Roger declined to rehash the event in detail but did state that as of our speaking he was convinced what he had seen was not a ghost, demonic entity, extraterrestrial or "cryptid" in the traditional sense. He stated confidently that the creatures were the result of a government breeding program, the details of which he had become privy to in the years following the 1982 incident. He mentions a man named Walt, who was connected to the aforementioned program. He also explains that he does not believe modern day visitors to the LBL are in danger of encountering a "Dogman," and that your average visitor is more likely to be attacked by a "rabid chipmunk."

Our conversation is brief, and he concludes by wishing us luck in our research and safe travels during our visit.

All Things Being Equal

Opinions vary within the community as to the validity of Roger's account as much as they do regarding the Massacre event itself. Perhaps the chief concern amongst detractors is his reticence to share his own last name or the last name of the family in question. While protecting his own identity makes quite a bit of sense in the age of the terroristic practice known as doxxing, the last name of the family might provide researchers with the opportunity to corroborate, at least in some capacity, the finer points of his testimony.

While that information has not been released to the public, Roger did share the family's surname with Elijah and Johnny prior to their recorded interview. Johnny explains that he will honor Roger's wish to keep the information private, but that the Cryptid Studies Institute team did cross reference the name they were given with common surnames in the LaGrange, Indiana area. The name Roger gave them was amongst the top three results.

Between filming sessions for *Dogman Territory: Werewolves of the Land Between the Lakes*, I and other members of the Small Town Monsters team undertook our own round of similar detective work. By consulting publicly available information we searched for land ownership records, birth and death certificates, relevant news stories and any other details we thought may be helpful, and cross referenced them against the three most common names in the LaGrange area. Heather Moser's access to a variety of document repositories, provided by her position as a college professor, opened in particular several avenues of research unavailable to the average armchair investigator. One might envision a half dozen people huddled around a living room, scattered across couches and armchairs and improvised seating, frantically typing away at laptops and touchscreens, calling out leads, one person picking up one and another the next, while results are shouted into the mix with equal fervor. While this played out, I could not help but liken myself to the protagonist of any number of whodunnit style creature features, wherein the star-studded cast find themselves in the film's proverbial war room, minutes away from a dramatic discovery and the film's final, climatic act. This is the scene as I recall it, but sadly, these investigative deep dives were not filmed.

Of the records consulted, we were not able to locate any documents relevant to a family of four with the names Levi, Dianne, Steven and Fannie and/or Connie in LaGrange during the 70s or 80s. One member of our team pointed out that even if the family's birth and death records were within the confines of the Amish community, that records of the property they owned outside the Amish area would still be available publicly. If a family of four never returned from a cross-country trip, their home would have been left to decay and eventually an investigation would have ensued. Even in remote areas, an abandoned residential property would, at some point, catch the attention of neighbors and government officials. After all, the property taxes would have gone unpaid.

I encourage the reader, once again, to draw their own conclusions. This fact alone does not invalidate Roger's story, and there are any number of mundane explanations to account for the absence of public records in any situation. A fun anecdote amongst those who have undertaken deep research into their genealogy (at least in the pre-internet age) is that when contacting courthouses and city halls in search of familial records, many are told that the documents they seek were long ago lost in a fire. A professor I studied under in college said that this is very often an excuse to save the clerk from having to dig through old boxes of documents, and that persistence is key when trying to map out one's ancestry. This alone may be the cause of the absence of available records.

As we have already learned, the story of the massacre itself predates the internet age and even Barton Nunnelly's *Hunt the Dogman*. It turns out locals have indeed been whispering about the beast of the LBL in the area for much longer. We will recall that Mike Smith heard the story in high school, as early as 1989. This nearly eliminates the possibility of the case being a fabrication of the internet age (CERN - the *Conseil Européen pour la Recherche Nucléaire* or European Council for Nuclear Research in English - would not release the world wide web into the hands of the public until 1993). As far as breeding programs of strange canines are concerned, this is another piece of the story which bleeds into the angle of government conspiracy, making it difficult to research or verify. As we learned early on, breeding programs are in use to re-introduce red wolves into the

Land Between the Lakes, but this would not likely be considered a parallel.

An Attempt at Conclusions

Opinions as to the nature of this story are as diverse as the wildlife of the Land Between the Lakes. Jessi and Joe Doyle would admit that when they first began their research into it, "We thought it was an internet invention,"

Their opinions would change, however, as would my own.

If there were four unrecorded deaths in the Land Between the Lakes in 1983, then it would be an event consistent with what other area researchers have mentioned in other cases. We can cite the testimonies of Martin Groves and Elijah Henderson as examples, wherein they mentioned numerous anecdotes of persons lost or killed under mysterious circumstances. The absence of public records, newspaper articles or news broadcasts covering the event would seem like an impossible obstacle to overcome when trying to verify a story's veracity, but as we've also heard, there seems to be a particular reticence on the part of local and/or federal government officials to disclose or discuss the potential reality behind the rumors of canine strangeness in the Land Between the Lakes.

If, however, a cover-up is in fact in play, its effectiveness would seem subjective. How, without any publicly verifiable records, has this story held up to so much scrutiny?

I'll invoke what I like to consider the Writer's Privilege, and state on the record that I believe *something* happened to give rise to this most grisly of Dogman-centric tales. On my skeptical days, I assume a family of four was on a pleasant spring camping trip, when one or more of them had a run in with a squirrel, or perhaps a raccoon. Perhaps they reported an animal attack, and the creature in question morphed from a squirrel to a coyote to a wolf to a bear, and at some point, after retelling, a werewolf.

This, however, seems an unlikely evolution. Why would a run-of-the-mill encounter with local wildlife merit such consistent and detailed preservation? And where did the gorier details - bodies in trees and a firefight lost against inhuman horrors - originate? This is only my own two proverbial cents, filtered through the lens of my own experiences and biases. While speaking with Jeremiah Byron, host of *The Bigfoot Society* podcast, during the interview phase of this volume, he provided a succinct anecdote which serves as an apt footnote to this case.

"I hope that a family did not actually have such a grisly demise in the LBL. But years of interviewing individuals has shown me that accounts such as this can easily be true."

Eli Watson, who was present throughout my visit to the LBL and whom I have consulted with regularly on this topic, provides a perspective that I am abashed to admit had not previously crossed my mind.

"Regardless of my own beliefs on the massacre itself, or whether it happened or not, it cannot be denied that the story has changed details based on who is telling the story. I would not be surprised to see that the story will change again in the upcoming years in response to the Small Town Monsters media attention of it. The story itself has the makings of a modern myth, from the family with no name, to the history of the location they were in, to the finding of the little girl's body. All these factors point to a story shrouded in mystery with answers that will never be found, but perhaps the truth is not in the facts of the massacre.

"There definitely are trustworthy sightings of werewolf-like creatures in the LBL, but the people there are not very open about it. In fact, the creation of the LBL itself suggests exactly this type of culture. A culture of people who prefer to stick to themselves and not bother with any overarching control, and even some resentment towards that power. The story of the massacre happening to a family is no insignificant detail, as many families were displaced when the TVA arrived. The LBL massacre, at its heart, is the story of a family that is torn to shreds by an unstoppable and evil force, then subsequently covered up and forgotten by the world. It is hard not to draw parallels between the history of the LBL and the story itself, and it suggests that more than being factually true, the massacre is a myth that truthfully explores, in ways only myths and legends can do, how a culture feels."

The topic of displacement and removal is a theme we will revisit throughout this text. It hints at something deeper than simple monster sightings, and Eli's connection of this concept to the story of the massacre itself is a significant lynchpin in this exploration. But once again, I'm getting ahead of myself.

Finally, Shannon LeGro contributes the following point of view, "I do think something untoward happened out there, but to what extent, and the culprit... will likely never be determined. Whether it's true or not though, it's a story that will forever be connected to Dogman lore and mentioned as yet another reason to avoid them."

I can conclude only with an assumption I made at the beginning of my research, not just for this book, but since Dogman sauntered through the headlights of my own line of sight. Like a dog chasing my own tail, and despite immeasurable interest, research, and investigation of this case, I'm somewhat at peace settling on the following statement:

There's more to the story than we know.

11
Sasquatch of The Lakes

It is impossible to discuss cryptozoology without mentioning Bigfoot.

I've tried. I've tried to explain what I write books about without saying, "you know, stuff like Bigfoot," but inevitably, it requires this qualifier to explain to most laypersons what a "Dogman researcher" does day to day. Long periods of poring over existing reports and short bouts of adrenaline when new information surfaces or a new lead takes shape highlight the lifestyle, but this can be difficult to impart.

The Land Between the Lakes is similar in this way, but unlike my inability to succinctly describe my profession, it is because the LBL has as much to be said about Bigfoot within its borders as it does the archetypal werewolf. Much more research is needed in the area to create a clearer picture, but we will examine a few encounters to at least provide additional context.

We have twice spoken with Mike Smith, who has spent his life in and around the Land Between the Lakes. In addition to potential run-ins with the LBL Dogmen, Mike has also experienced at least one visual encounter with our well-loved human-adjacent cryptid.

Lake Barkley

It was an idyllic day on Lake Barkley when Mike and his family set out on a fishing trip. It was cool and windy, and their usual boat ramp was closed. Mike knew of a less-frequented ramp nearby and utilized it to make a berth on the surface of the lake.

They ate lunch by the lakeside, choosing an isolated location. Before long, they heard what sounded like footsteps.

"It was about sixty-eight yards away. What was neat about it was I said 'oh —-, there's bigfoot, you know, cussing around my kids, but when that happens to you...'"

Something large and alive moved in the brush. An upright, shaggy form with brown fur, moving along the shore, not breaking its line of sight with the boat.

"There were trees shaking up there. We think there were two of them."

Mike reflects on how the sighting made him feel.

"I wasn't that scared of it. I was in awe. I felt pretty safe in the boat. So, we drifted down the bank, just kind of collecting our thoughts. My oldest daughter did see the tree shaking, and they were trees this big around."

Mike indicates a circle roughly the size of a large dinner plate with his hands. Soon came the more sounds, this time the apparent voice of whatever was disturbing the forest.

"A frustrated, gutteral *whoop*."

Mike's wife was shaken, concerned the creature might be waiting by their truck when they reached it. Thankfully, this was not the case.

The area of Mike's sighting has been further investigated, yielding loud knocking sounds at night like what Mike and his family heard. Mike speculates that the hot dogs his family prepared for lunch may have drawn the creatures to the area.

"I think it's like bears and sharks and everything else. There's probably some bad ones, and I know there are people that have had some bad experiences. But the area I'm in, I don't think they want to hurt you."

Mike continues, "I've had five other sightings since then. I've heard some screams and had some other interactions."

There would not be time during our conversation to examine these additional encounters, but the one described above does more than make the point - Sasquatch lives in the LBL.

We have also met Martin Groves, who would describe in detail witnessing a pair of Sasquatch-like creatures appearing in conjunction with a pair of upright canines in 1993. Elijah Henderson would mention during our conversations that based on the reports he has examined, Sasquatch activity generally seems to be concentrated in the southern areas of the park, while Dogman activity is more prevalent in the north. From this we might infer that Sasquatch prefers Tennessee while Dogman is partial to Kentucky, but an exact set of metrics to support this idea is unavailable. Both anecdotes, one coming from a detailed eyewitness encounter, indicates that the two creatures seem to have *some* sort of interconnected relationship, even if only by proximity. To speculate further on the nature of this relationship, more data is needed regarding the nature of the entities in question.

Sasquatch is regarded by a not-insignificant portion of the research community as an unclassified hominid. An ape. A flesh and blood species which, by means we have yet to fully ascertain, evades capture and mainstream scientific identification. There are theories of a more outlandish nature, such as a potential UFO connection or perhaps a spiritual or interdimensional being making fleeting appearances in our reality, but we risk too much digression from the point.

Dogman is, as we will continue to learn, a thing that regularly subverts and defies the expectations of both flesh and blood cryptid encounters and spectral or otherworldly activity.

It seems to toe the line between both worlds, at least given our meager understanding of each. While I risk saying this too often, we will return to this point in much greater detail at a more appropriate time.

Public Data

A well-known resource for reporting and researching Bigfoot activity is the publicly available database of the Bigfoot Field Researchers Organization, or the BFRO for short. Report #33322, a citation for which is provided in the relevant portion of this book, describes a sighting in a strikingly familiar location - the town of Cadiz, where I would spend the duration of my visit to the area while not inside the park.

The witness describes leaving the Lake Barkley resort, traveling by vehicle at approximately 50 miles per hour. They saw what they at first thought to be a large tree by the side of the road, but which soon revealed itself to be something else entirely. Specifically, the figure was "running."

It stood approximately seven feet tall, its head above the roof of the witness's minivan, and had a brow which is specifically qualified as "neanderthal" with a "flatish [sic]" nose.

This report would receive additional follow up by the BFRO, and commentary by investigator Mary

Mallon states, "The encounter took place not far from the Land Between the Lakes National Recreation Area, where there have been numerous sightings of Bigfoot and the Beast of LBL."

Beyond the Park

The reasons for Bigfoot to be in the LBL are the same as any other area in which Bigfoot seems to hang out. Plenty of space, an infinite number of hiding places, ready access to food (depending on what Bigfoot eats), ample water. The LBL presents a unique advantage to the enterprising Sasquatch, as firearms are prohibited almost entirely. It is not likely that Bigfoot is aware of this fact, but as with all the rest, we can only speculate.

This presents, once again, a striking overlap with other areas bearing consistent Dogman sightings - Sam Houston National Forest, located on the outskirts of Houston, Texas, is a prime example. Sasquatch and Dogman reports have been thick in Sam Houston for generations, and my conversations with a few of the locals in 2022 revealed to me that the breadth and density of their frequency is vastly under-appreciated by the research community. They are a known element to many of those that live in the area, accepted as a part of the environment. The Land Between the Lakes presents a vivid parallel.

The phenomenon extends well beyond the borders of the park as well. At the conclusion of my visit, Aleksandar Petakov would drop Shannon LeGro and I off at the Nashville Airport before proceeding to Anderson County, KY. He was slated to revisit the location where he had captured thermal footage of a large animal moving in the tree line only a year before. His investigation is detailed in full in the YouTube video *Bigfoot - Beyond the Trail: Central Kentucky Sasquatch Investigation.*

Comparisons

The comparisons between Dogman and Sasquatch are an essential part of the discussion. Joe Doyle provides a comment which succinctly describes their separation, making a point I've often returned to when asked after the same.

"With sasquatch, people will have these encounters, and it changes their lives in one way or another. It was either horrifying, or they have like a spiritual kind of awakening with it. They feel more in touch with nature, they just feel like they've come alive after the sighting. You don't get that with Dogman. You get that it's always overwhelmingly negative. Even if it's just how terrified they were at the sighting, and sometimes it goes even further than that."

This is hardly even a beginning to a proper bout of Sasquatch research. Were unclassified apes the focus of this work, dozens of additional reports and anecdotes may have been included. But as Bigfoot has a place in the Land Between the Lakes, so also must he have one here. For now, however, we will leave Bigfoot to his own devices. We're looking for something scarier.

12
The Fog - 2023

Martin Groves' first encounter with the upright dogs of the LBL, taking place in the 1990s, has captured the attention of the research community since it was first shared in the film *American Werewolves*. Were it his only account, it would still be a dramatic and impactful case. After a second encounter, just over a year past at time of writing, the saga of Martin's run-ins with the creatures takes on additional traces of strangeness that confound with renewed complexity. This report also bears a potential link to the ancient world, when our ancestors believed in monsters, and may be the relative of something recorded by ancient Indian scribes before the dawn of modern civilization. Or it may not.

A Second Encounter

In October of 2022, Martin was on a regular trip through the park, traveling by pickup truck along an isolated, dirt road. It was a narrow path connecting to The Trace near Mt. Pleasant Cemetery, only a few miles from the location of Martin's first sighting. On one side the road dissolves into underbrush which, after several dozen yards, gives way to a steep incline. On the other side is a sharp drop-off - a creek or gully, easily over seven feet in depth, which snakes its way off into the trees parallel to and away from the road. There's no cell reception here, no unnatural light sources. Nothing save the dirt road to indicate that people have ever been in this place, and even that has been left to deteriorate in recent years.

Martin was not unaccompanied during his second encounter. He'd brought a friend, another frequenter of the LBL wilds. Conveniently for our purposes, this individual would also witness the creature and vouch for its existence.

Darrell Denton is a long-time resident of the area. Much like Martin, he is well known and greatly respected, having served for many years as a public servant. Darrell is a former mayor and alderman and became acquainted with Martin before the lawman's retirement. In fact, their initial meeting took place decades before, when Martin was dispatched to investigate what essentially amounts to sasquatch activity on Darrell's property.

The men drove along the dirt road, windows down, taking in the scenery and the cool night air. This was a place they'd visited many times, and when they led the STM film crew and me back to the spot to relay the encounter, they were able to locate it without hesitation.

Something in the underbrush, on the vehicle's passenger side caught their attention. Something moved, crawling, ascending from the gully which banked off from the trail.

Darrell saw it first.

It was a sprawling, hairy form, moving on four legs in a spider-crawl. A canine shape, with elongated limbs. There was no visible tail, and the creature's appearance was accompanied by a hazy fog which belied the otherwise pleasant weather. We are reminded of the recurring presence of mist mentioned by Eric Mintel in the Bray Road area as recently as 2022.

The creature itself glowed with a blueish luminescence. The glow was separate from the running lights of the vehicle, and as I would soon see for myself, the area is bereft of lighting installations of any sort. The glow seemed to emanate from the entity's fur and eyes, bright enough to be seen in the waning twilight. Even stranger, the creature's body was noticeably translucent - details of the brush beneath and behind it could be seen through its black-gray fur.

The creature crossed the road, rising on to two legs, and made a hasty retreat into the woods on the other side. It crashed into the trees and seemed to leap up the side of the ridge in only a few impossible strides, before disappearing over the top.

In its wake, it left behind an odor which both Darrell and Martin describe as the worst thing either of them have smelled. Martin cites his experience working on crime scenes, where truly horrifying events have left every type of unpleasant odor imaginable. He describes this as being far worse. The odor had an immediate effect on both men, prompting nausea and disorientation, as if a chemical weapon had been uncapped on the narrow roadway.

They left the area, as quickly as their disorientation and the unpaved road would allow. At time of writing, the glowing wolfman has not made another appearance - at least not one of which I am aware.

It would, however, leave a souvenir behind. Martin's vehicle, a standard size pickup truck, was coated in a sticky residue. The debilitating odor which both men describe was thick on the stuff, and it was hastily washed off to prevent further contamination.

To call this encounter outlandish might seem an understatement.

A translucent being, hinting at something spiritual in nature, yet which interacts with the physical environment. Luminescence which should be impossible. A wolf life visage. The appearance of fog or smoke as a herald of the creature's appearance. Lingering physical effects, and trace evidence in the form of an unidentified, possibly organic substance on the witnesses' vehicle.

While this might seem a cryptid encounter on par with the most bizarre that we can compare it to - The Flatwoods Monster incident comes to mind, as a noxious odor was one aspect of that encounter - there may be hints of a creature like this one in the annals of Indian mythology.

We will briefly return to *The Book of Werewolves*, but like many citations originating with that text, a much older piece of literature serves as the primary source.

The Rakshasa

The Rakshasa is a demonic entity in classical Indian texts. It makes appearances in the *Bhagavad Gita*, mentioned as a malicious demon which is beholden to the power and authority of more benevolent gods. In the *Mahabharata*, the term "Rakshasa" appears over *1200 times*. One quote from the text states,

"For what sin are beings, when they fall from heaven, attacked by these fierce and sharp-toothed Rakshasas?"

It is described in ferocious terms, and Sabine Baring-Gould summarized the creature thusly in *The Book of Werewolves*.

From Baring-Gould's original text:

Râkshasa is "a misshapen giant 'like to a cloud,' with a red beard and red hair, with pointed teeth, ready to lacerate and devour human flesh. His body is covered with coarse bristling hair, his huge mouth open, he looks from side to side as he walks, lusting after the flesh and blood of men, to satisfy his raging hunger, and quench his consuming thirst. Towards nightfall his strength increases manifold. He can change his shape at will. He haunts the woods, and roams howling through the jungle; in short, he is to the Hindu what the werewolf is to the European"

Not exactly a point for point match to Martin and Darrell's description, but one with striking similarities all the same. A creature which descends in a fog or in the shape of a cloud, can shapeshift and hunt after human beings in the wild places. A malicious entity mentioned throughout sacred texts as an unfriendly, demonic spirit. Does the Rakshasa - or something like it - yet dwell in the bizarre realm of the Land Between the Lakes?

It may be a stretch to make this assumption, but to find precedent for a creature resembling the subject of Martin and Darrell's sighting, and with such specific parallels to boot, in the pages of ancient mythology is something which must at least be considered. The Rakshasa and its ilk certainly warrant further study; what other connections to contemporary paranormal phenomena might we find by consulting the classical writings of ancient people? Very often study of the werewolf phenomenon seems to find itself confined to European and North American accounts. Mesopotamia, South America, and as we now see, India are also places where bipedal shapeshifters have been recorded.

It must be stated that a proper examination of this idea is not present here. Baring-Gould's comparison comes from his frame of reference as a white European Christian in the 1700s. Consultation with a scholar of Indian literature, as well as an expert on Indian folkloric traditions and religious beliefs, has not been conducted in the writing of this volume. Time constraints sadly prevented this, and without it, the possible correlation can only be speculated on.

The Search Continues

In 2023, Martin confesses that his hunt for the creature has not ended.

He now ventures into the woods at night, alone - much to the chagrin of his friends and family - armed only with a kerosene lamp and an emergency GPS tracker. His hope is to replicate, in some fashion, his original encounter with the creatures.

"I have to know," he says. I commented during our conversation that it seems this search has become an extremely personal journey for him - many of us enter into the paranormal field as hobbyists or casual onlookers, but Martin's journey has been very different. In explaining why, he says quite simply,

"I don't want another hundred dead."

He believes that there is true danger in the park which the vast majority of its visitors are blissfully unaware of, or perhaps, unwilling to believe in. Martin, however, stands by his assertion with an iron resolve. Recalling his first - and not final - encounter with the Dogmen of The Lakes, he remembers an impression which has stuck with him for over thirty years.

"A feeling of evil that cannot be described."

This part of our conversation took place on the exact spot of Martin's initial encounter. By flashlight and from memory, Martin led our group into the thicket, off the trail and down into the gully where he and his hunting partner first encountered both the Dogmen of The Lakes and something they could only describe as Sasquatch. The details of the location correlate to his story without deviation.

In summary, Martin Groves is the type of witness/expert that every paranormal researcher clamors after. An established, documented, and respectable reputation. Years of data recorded empirically and with attention to detail. A strong knowledge of the area in question. Training and experience which enable them to filter their findings objectively and then present it to an interested party without embellishment. I may not understand what Martin and Darrell experienced (I certainly don't), but if I may risk exposing too much of my own bias, I would say this:

I believe them.

Addendum: More Lights in the Sky

We touched briefly on UFO sightings in chapter 3, and a teaser was left concerning a spike in reports. It was in October of 2022, when Martin and Darrell's run-in took place, that UFO encounters in Kentucky and Tennessee would seem to increase exponentially. According to the NUFORC database, 14 sightings would come in from Tennessee and an additional 6 from Kentucky in October of 2022. By contrast, Tennessee saw 10 sightings in September and only 5 in November. Kentucky bore 4 sightings in September and 3 in November.

If that's too many numbers for you (it is for me), then perhaps a simpler breakdown will help (it did for me). For both states, the total of sightings flows thusly:

September - 14 total sightings
October - 20 total sightings - Martin and Darrell's encounter
November - 8 total sightings

We must, *must* reiterate that correlation does not prove causation. This may be pure coincidence, and perhaps I risk too much ridicule for including too many disparate points and phenomena in this chapter. But it is the bizarre nature of what Darrell and Martin saw, and in truth, the Dogman question itself, which continually seems to lend itself to further extrapolation and hypotheses. I am certain I will never know the answer to what happened in October of 2022, but I'll break character once more and admit that of all the cases I've researched, this one ranks amongst the most compelling and confounding.

13
The Footprint - 2020

"You mentioned 'other stuff,'" I said, and asked about the nature of the "other stuff."

During the first half of our interview, Mike Smith would state in no uncertain terms that there are parts of the Land Between the Lakes that he no longer visits. Despite this, he continues to research and investigate the strange goings on in the park, even including his family in the endeavor. On November 8th of 2020 Mike ventured out with his son and would record one of the most compelling pieces of physical evidence relevant to our discussion that I've ever encountered.

Mike would first investigate the location in question with a witness.

"We went out at night. And a guy had a sighting, and we were down past the sighting with another guy that was there."

Another anecdotal Dogman report had found its way into Mike's inbox a few days before, and he had decided to follow up on the story by exploring the area.

"I'm trying to learn," he says simply.

He has examined numerous areas bearing trace evidence on previous expeditions and describes the way in which these apparently large creatures seem to bend and break limbs well above the eye level of any human being. If they are indeed six or more feet tall on average, the removal of high brush might allow for greater visibility and easier passage through the trees.

"I've noticed, if you look up - these things are big."

He continues, "If you want to see where they've been, look up high. You can see tree breaks and twists, where I think they're just clearing stuff out of their way."

Mike also mentions the knee-high grass and undergrowth which permeates the LBL's off road areas, another obstacle which seems to provide little resistance to whatever is living there.

"That's nothing to these things."

This was the type of evidence Mike may have expected to encounter. What he found instead would prove far more dramatic.

"It was night, and we were close to the camp, and we got down in the bottom of this ravine, and we heard - we thought it was some of the garbled speak, like you hear about bigfoot. I mean there was a sound down there. It wasn't scary then, but it was like, 'let's get back.'"

He would return to the site a week later.

"The next weekend I took my son. And he was skeptical - we went out, and he's satisfied now that I'm not crazy.

"We went down to this old cemetery."

Mike describes feeling an odd presence in the burial ground. It's a feeling most people have likely experienced at least once or twice, common in graveyards, abandoned buildings, and other liminal places.

Mike and his son soon found themselves at the tombstone of Richard Bannister, a murder victim, interred in the 1930s. The pair had brought along a K2 EMF meter, a tool commonly used in ghost investigations and were taking readings in the cemetery near Bannister's grave.

"Wind was blowing, and we got in the truck, built a fire, talked on the K2 a little bit, and we heard something."

They heard walking. Not just random rustling and stirring of branches, but distinguishable footfalls in the leaves.

"In my experience, the Sasquatch, they watch you. I think there's always two of them, at least. They don't come down, they stay up."

Whatever had just made itself known behaved differently.

"But we heard this thing coming, and we said okay, let's just stay here, something's walking through the woods. And you can tell, the [sound of] bipedal, you can tell the difference between a deer, or whatever."

Standing in the cemetery, the footsteps could be heard moving around the perimeter.

Mike and his son returned to the truck, and then heard bizarre, guttural, speech-like noises coming from the dark.

"You feel it more than you hear it."

The scene took on a tangible sense of danger. Mike explains, "I don't like crowds. I don't like going to places where I feel like I'm being herded like cattle. I definitely don't like being stalked. And I looked at my son, and I said, 'Okay. Let's get in the truck.'"

Mike doesn't purport that the area in question is necessarily Dogman Territory but has experienced enough to make at least a few assertions.

"I've confidently known something was close. I should be able to see it, and it's gone. There's something out there that's big that can disappear."

Shannon would ask an important question at this juncture.

"That area that you get a bad feeling from - what about during the day? Is it a different feeling at night?"

"No, I got the feeling during the day. I didn't have any knowledge of this place I'd been in connection with Dogman. I just knew I didn't want to be there."

Mike would return to the cemetery a third time. This time he brought along additional tools in his field kit, amongst them the ingredients necessary for creating plaster casts. He would get lucky, finding an odd indentation in the ground right on top of where the strange noises seemed to be coming from. I was fortunate enough to examine the cast when I spoke with Mike in 2023.

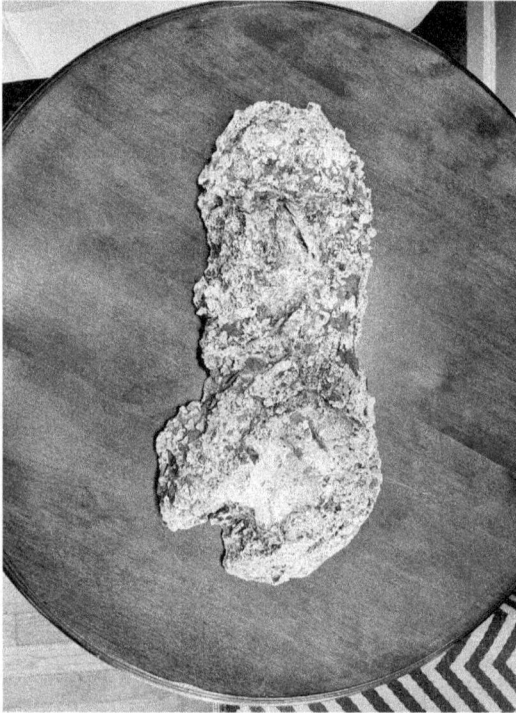

A print found in the Land Between the Lakes in 2020, cast by Mike Smith. Photo by the author.

The print is right at sixteen inches in length. Its width is beyond a handbreadth by at least thirty percent - seven inches at the widest point - and the cast itself is solid and heavy. Mike points out a distinct arch and what appears to be an elongated protrusion - perhaps a toe - on one side. Like most prints cast in pursuit of strange creatures it leaves the imagination to fill in the details amidst the impressions of brush and soil, but in my opinion, its size and shape preclude a human being or fallen tree limb as the source. Mike makes no claim to have captured an actual Dogman print, and neither will I claim to have examined a cast of one.

The possibility, however, cannot be ignored.

After our interview, Mike was kind enough to send me a video he took of the print before casting it. The details of the cast seem more vivid after examining the footage, and the one minute forty-nine second clip provides a detailed breakdown of the height, width, depth and key features, including what appears to be a midtarsal break. My initial assumption - that this is not an easily identifiable cast of some known animal - is further validated, at least in my own mind.

Still images taken from the video provided by Mike Smith to the author. 1) the print's full 16-inch length is shown next to a measuring tape 2) the print's depth is measured at almost three inches 3) the "toe"

Some will take one look at this cast and immediately write it off as a Sasquatch print, and I will give that there's room for this line of speculation. The vocalizations Mike heard seem similar to those reported in many Sasquatch encounters - might Mike and his son have run across a primate-template cryptid instead of a canine one?

It's entirely possible. If so, however, we are presented with another case of Sasquatch making appearances in the wake of purported Dogman encounters. After all, Mike visited the area in the first place while investigating a Dogman report corroborated by at least two witnesses. I am immediately reminded of Martin Groves' report of witnessing pairs of Sasquatch and Dogmen in the 1990s, and again of Elijah Henderson's sighting of two colors of eyeshine in an area he calls the Dark Hollow. But there's a problem here, despite conjecture. The print bears very little resemblance to any generally accepted Sasquatch print casts that I personally have ever seen.

In addition, and far more significant than my own opinion, Mike states that he shared the images of the print and the cast with well-known and highly respected Sasquatch researcher Dr. Jeff Meldrum, author of *Sasquatch: Legend Meets Science*. Mike says that Mr. Meldrum stated unequivocally that the print is not, in his opinion, one which belongs to a Sasquatch.

Shannon asks one final question of Mr. Smith - given the opportunity, would he want to see one - to have a real-life visual encounter with this thing called Dogman?

"If I went and never saw one and I could just focus on fishing... that's what I would prefer."

14
The Dark - 2019

Elijah Henderson of the Cryptid Studies Institute, who one will note is quoted frequently within this text, experienced his own encounter very near the area of Martin's initial sighting. This would occur in 2019.

It is my habit to extract quotes from the people I interview and summarize their stories in my own words. I do this for several reasons, one of which is to avoid being accused of lazy writing, but in Elijah's case I have made an exception. He provided an account which was so detailed (and so well written) that not to share it in its original form seemed a tragic waste. It is below, in its original and unaltered form.

"You had asked me if I had any strange encounters of my own in the park, and while I have not had the opportunity to witness a Dogman or a sasquatch with my own eyes, I have had an unusual thing or two occur while in the park. Me and my family went down to an area with a history of Dogman activity, and it is actually where the body of the "bowhunter" was found in a soybean field. We nickname this area

Dark Hollow, and it has been one of the better places in the park to do nighttime outings. It is here where we have brought other friends and researchers, and have heard unusual howls, and noises throughout the night. On this specific trip with my family however, we had arrived with the intention of tent camping through the night, and as the evening settled in, we quickly realized that there was an abundance of cotton mouth snakes (this area is right around a creek), and we ended up counting either 5-6 of these snakes. My mother didn't mind the idea of Dogman, or sasquatch, but she quickly drew the line at snakes and we started to pack up and make our way back to the house. My Dad knew I wasn't ready to leave so we decided that we would sit around the camp bathed in the glow of multiple fiery tiki torches and listen to see if anything would stir up.

During the process of packing up the gear, my Dad noticed a set of orange eyeshine on the opposite bank, and we had a trail camera set up over there anyway so across the creek we went. We actually had to pass a cotton mouth coiled up in the path on the way over, and once over, we realized that it was nothing more than a raccoon. But as we were shining out flashlights into the woods I noticed some eye shine, and this shine had a blue appearance to it. A lot of Dogman reports describe the eye shine as having an electric blue glow to it, and this was also a blue color. I brought it to my Dad's attention, and pointed out where it was coming from in between two trees, and he said: "Where? Right where that really dark spot is?" As soon as he said that there was a very deep grunt or growl, and something smacked one of the trees where that "dark spot" was coming from. Whatever it was, hit with enough force that this medium-sized tree started swaying; and my Dad, being the protective father that he was, then put a hand over my chest and gradually started backing us away from the woods where this occurred, back past the coiled up cottonmouth (which was arguably worse than what had just happened) and then back across the creek to camp. We couldn't leave at this point, things were really starting to get good, so bathed in the glow of some tiki torches, we sat down and merely listened to our environment. After a few minutes my Dad asked me if I still had the silent dog whistle in my pocket, and I did so I began to puff on the whistle, however it didn't sound like it was tuned quite correctly, so I gave another puff on it. And after exactly forty seconds, something began to rip and tear through the woods in our direction, it sounded just like a T-Rex coming through the forest breaking branches and limbs to come after us. I actually have an audio recording of the moment this happened, and you can hear the limbs snapping and breaking. Needless to say, after this we called it quits, packed up our tiki torches, and got out of there. What's funny is that once we left the South entrance, we stopped at a gas station for drinks and casually brought up the "beast of LBL" to the attendant who had certainly heard of the legend before.

That would be the most intense event that I have ever been present for, however we do a lot of outings there in that park and I'm always hoping for something greater to happen. I'm just waiting for that highly coveted Dogman sighting to happen in Land Between the Lakes, and I'm confident that If I am diligent and keep visiting, I will someday get it, and perhaps, once I see it, I will wish I had not!"

My sincere thanks to Elijah for providing such a detailed account. My own writing preferences aside, sometimes a direct testimony from a witness is the best form of presentation.

There are a few interesting pieces to pick apart in this event.

The eye shine Elijah mentions - first orange, then later blue - indicates that SOMETHING was at the perimeter of the Hendersons' campsite. The varying colors described may indicate *more than one kind* of creature, and while I risk too much confirmation bias, I cannot help but think of Martin Groves' encounter in 1993.

The audio Elijah mentions is indeed striking as well. Alarming, even, if one imagines themselves in the woods after dark while hearing it. The description of a T-Rex tearing through the underbrush is an apt one. The reader is encouraged to seek out the YouTube video *"The Beast of LBL - Dark Hollow - Nightmare Nuggets of Cryptid Terror"* from the Cryptid Studies Institute.

Some reading this will point to the description of what may have been a wood knock and categorize this as a more likely Sasquatch encounter. I can hardly disprove this, but synchronicity leaves us at least some room to extrapolate further. The encounter took place, as Elijah said, near the location where a hunter was allegedly found dead over 20 years before. An area of purportedly repeated Dogman activity. And, most striking to the author, the appearance of two colors of eyeshine, which opens up a wealth of possibilities.

Most importantly, it is yet another stark case of human beings crossing paths with the inexplicable things that lurk in the dark. Large beasts in the forests of the LBL, seeming to defy easy identification by even the most experienced outdoor adventurers.

15
The Crossing – 2023

Elijah Henderson and his father are not the only members of the Henderson clan to encounter odd things in the LBL. Elijah's sister, Gabby, who I also met in November of 2023, had what I generally refer to as an "a-typical" sighting in May of that year. Gabby is an integral part of the Cryptid Studies Institute's work, and her encounter provides valuable insight. The story she would share with us also took place very, very recently, making it the most recent relevant sighting to come out of the LBL at time of writing (to my knowledge).

On May 6th of 2023, the Cryptid Studies Institute team was on a research trip in the LBL. As Elijah has mentioned, this is a regular outing for the group, and they carried their usual array of investigative and outdoor gear. They would end up not needing it, at least not for what was about to take place. Elijah and Gabby were accompanied by a few of their fellow researchers and had split into smaller groups to make the trip by car into the park proper.

Weather records indicate clear skies, with zero precipitation. The average temperature was around 63 degrees, with a low of 53. Gabby mentions that the moon was nearly full, which is also corroborated by lunar phase records available online. It was shortly before midnight, well into the evening, when the sighting occurred. A storm was on its way in, and Gabby states that the night was "alive" with numerous deer and other wildlife sightings.

As they traveled by vehicle along the Trace, something would catch the group's eye. A figure would crawl across the road, illuminated by the headlines of the vehicle.

Gabby's estimation is that it was around six feet in length, lanky, with bear-like fur. The creature was visible for ten to thirty seconds from about ten yards, though size and distance can be difficult to estimate in the dark. The group was close enough to make out a muzzled snout and pointed ears. The creature also had what Gabby describes as a concave spine, "Like a man."

It was quick. Gabby says the creature moved, "so fast," and that its movements were measured and stealthy, "The way a beast moves."

The creature would complete its road crossing before disappearing into the brush, leaving the witnesses startled, continuing about unknown business.

I asked her point blank - "what do you think you saw?"

She hesitated a moment before responding, but in the same factual, measured tone said, "I believe it was a Dogman."

She was also not the only witness. Another of the team's group, a friend of the Hendersons, also saw the creature as it passed through the headlights.

Gabby would also state that she felt "excited" by the sighting and does not mention being afraid or unsettled. It would be difficult not to feel some measure of excitement, one might guess. After countless hours spent documenting inactivity in the park, the rush of finally seeing something is a thrill I continue to chase myself. Gabby does not attempt to embellish or even sell us on whether this took place. She relays the events surrounding the night in question as she might relay to a barista how she takes her coffee.

One possible answer is that Gabby saw a "normal" animal and mistook it for something more. Detractors will immediately default to this explanation.

There are plenty of animals in and around the park which could account for such a sighting. Red wolves, coyotes, large dogs, bears, boars and plenty of other fauna inhabit the region.

The problem with this being a "regular animal" sighting comes from Gabby and her friend's familiarity with the local wildlife. While someone not accustomed to the wild reaches of the Land Between the Lakes might be likely to make this mistake, Gabby and her team are far more readily equipped to identify known species than many others (me included). The duration of the encounter was certainly sufficient to provide such an opportunity, were it possible at all. With a line of sight lasting up to half a minute, a trained eye would likely have little difficulty identifying a simple coyote. Cross referencing potential encounters with known animals is a regular part of the Cryptid Studies Institute's work, even if only anecdotally - my own conversations with Gabby and Elijah are a prime example. The presence of a second witness, who also felt they had witnessed something inexplicable, only adds fuel to a growing flame.

Gabby speaks factually and concisely about her sighting, giving direct answers to our varied questions. She also does an expert job of ignoring the cameras, a skill I am still trying to master. We would cross paths again on one of our later forays into the woods, and she would demonstrate additional skill in navigating the unstable ground, even as Shannon and I stumbled over loose branches and leaf-filled ruts.

Ms. Henderson's sighting is significant for a few reasons. First, it fits the profile of what many generally consider to be an "a-typical" Dogman sighting, in which the creature seems to be crossing the road, exposing itself out of necessity. This is a recurring pattern. I would examine no fewer than three similar reports during the writing of *The Texas Dogman Triangle,* and as we have discussed, the Beast of Bray Road was frequently seen by roadsides.

Secondly, Gabby's encounter comes from her perspective not only as someone familiar with the day-to-day of the Land Between the Lakes, but also with a deep grasp of the strangeness that surrounds it. Her ability to say "I believe it was a Dogman" should not be downplayed, as many witnesses in these cases are unable or unwilling to define specifically what they believe they have seen. Gabby has the research chops to make that call, and while she remained open to the possibility that she may have simply seen a large animal during our discussion, I found her conviction - and the unembellished way in which she shared the story - compelling in no small amount.

Third, and most obviously, it is yet another potential run in with the Dogmen of the Lakes in what is becoming a very long list. Perhaps additional sightings have occurred in the less-than-a-year (at time of writing) since this one but allow me to state my gratitude at being given the opportunity to research such a recent event. And one recorded by such an effective and credible witness.

16
Hunters

When making early notes for the drafting of this manuscript, I settled on the title near the beginning of the process. It was chosen based entirely on the profile of Dogman encounters I had hitherto researched or read about in the area, prior to my realization that the park was, in fact, a literal hunting ground used by Native American tribes. In this chapter we will discuss hunters of an altogether different nature.

The template of the Dogman many of us imagine is built around that of known wolves and dogs. Recurring descriptions generally lend themselves to this, except for the upright stance, but this may have a practical explanation. The anomalous physical feature which defies scientific reasoning is the glowing eyes, but we'll get there soon.

The arguments against the existence of Dogman are due their equal time. We learned early on of the skepticism which sets the tone for many relevant conversations, and identified the shortcomings of available evidence, both in quantity and veracity.

The zoological objections are likely the most significant.

It's easy to posit that an unidentified canine breed is hanging out in the wild in any given place. It happens all the time, in fact. Questions posed to veterinary professionals and cryptozoologists alike have yielded a variety of affirmative responses, at least allowing for the possibility that some of these sightings are the result of a biological canine amalgamation.

The difficult question becomes - why are they walking on two legs? Bipedal locomotion can be taught to and learned by canines. Spend an hour at any local dog park and one is likely to spot at least one example.

Behaviors and Physical Traits

The behavior exhibited by alleged Dogman entities in the Land Between the Lakes seems to hint at a predatory, aggressive, unfriendly nature. Canines are naturally built predators in the first place, but the way these Dogmen behave seems to emphasize the meaner tendencies of their apparent four-legged cousins.

A quick breakdown of canine anatomy is in order. They have forward facing eyes, allowing them to observe and see clearly with limited visibility. They have a keen sense of smell, many thousands of times better than that of any human. They can move quickly, quietly, and blend in with their environments.

Wolves and many dog breeds have triangular ears. They can perceive sounds from as far away as *ten miles* in some cases - *ten miles* - and their ears can move independently of one another.

They have lean, muscular builds, and in a natural environment are generally devoid of excess body mass. Large dog breeds can exceed 150 pounds, and in veterinary situations, generally require special handling to avoid injury to patients and medical staff.

A wolf pack will spread out and surround potential prey before engaging them, cutting off avenues of escape, assessing weaknesses and dangers. Very often a single wolf will seize large prey by the nose or neck, allowing its companions to present a unified assault. In cases of smaller animals, predatory canines will generally go for the neck, allowing for a quick kill.

A human being has an average maximum bite force of 120 pounds per square inch. That sounds impressive, until you consider that the average dog weighs in around 300 pounds per square inch. Wolves average around 400-500, but some studies state that a wolf in distress can issue more than *one thousand* pounds per square inch of pressure.

Were we to scale that up to a creature which stands more than six feet tall... well. I am without the scientific or mathematical credentials to make such a calculation, but the implications are staggering.

If the creatures of the Land Between the Lakes are, in fact, biological entities, then they represent what would seem to be an enhanced set of canine traits. An apparently muscular build hints at the powerful anatomy we see in classified canines. The pointed ears would give away all but the most silent of pursuers, and the glowing eyes might indicate a type of enhanced night vision - dogs have limited visibility in the dark, but not on the scale of many nocturnal animals.

The ability to walk upright might provide greater visibility in tall brush, which was touched on previously. Where this behavior would originate in any quadrupedal animal is anyone's guess, but a recent headline does provide us with at least one real world example.

In 2022 a couple in the United Kingdom captured video of a small animal in their garden (that's British for 'yard,' I've since learned). The animal was quite plainly a fox and was sniffing and rooting around in the grass as its species is wont to do. There was a problem, though - the fox only had two legs. This is not the plot of a children's story or animated film, but rather an *actual* two-legged canine. Granted, the creature was walking on its front legs, not the rear ones, as the front are the only ones present. The animal is clearly compensating for an injury or deformity. It can't be said that the fox in the video is walking "upright," necessarily, but it does raise its rear half when taking longer strides, orienting for balance. Its shorter steps show it keeping closer to the ground, almost moving the way it would if it were in possession of all four legs.

The Two-Legged Fox of Derbyshire

It may be a stretch to assume that this fox has anything to do with the Dogmen of the Lakes, but I would argue the inverse. I would argue that it proves the canine ability to walk on two legs in a natural setting. There are many other examples to be found if one goes looking, of dogs adapting to an apparent disability and living fairly normal lives. The special thing about this case is that this creature adapted to this behavior *in the wild*, without veterinary care or other apparent human intervention.

Environment

The environment of the LBL is ideal for anything - or anyone - who wishes to remain concealed. Observing the state of the park today, and speaking with locals and frequent visitors, reveals that upkeep has been lacking for quite some time. An absence of personnel - certainly a result of an absence of funding - has seen many of the roads go untended and unpatrolled. Many areas, both pre- and post-LBL, have simply been left to rot. My mind goes back to the ankle-deep garbage on the floor of one of the bunkers, and the abandoned fire watch tower we passed while driving along the Trace. The sheer amount of space - more than 170,000 acres - coupled with the staggeringly small number of eyes on it, precludes the idea that anything lurking in the LBL would be easy to suss out. Its legacy as a place of crime and death proves this, not even accounting for the repeated conjecture over paranormal phenomena. As we discussed early in this volume, The LBL Recreation and Heritage Act was passed in 2022, allotting an additional 8 million in annual funding to the park. It must be hoped that these funds will see at least a few more park rangers added to the ranks. Joe Doyle would explain during our interview in 2023 that, at present, there are only four.

The presence of water in the area is an obvious thing which almost need not be stated; it's in the name of the place. There is certainly no shortage of watering holes for any animal, predatory or otherwise. Dehydration would be the least of anyone's concerns, at least during the warmer months, and even the winter yields frozen bodies of water that could be penetrated to obtain a quick drink.

The park provides ample game for a predatory species. Deer, waterfowl, small mammals, and much more are in abundance. Wild turkey hunting is but one of many annual events. Also in the mix are wild hogs, which apparently appear in such great numbers, they must occasionally be culled through organized hunts (or, what is purported to be such).

The bones found in the underground tunnel by Jessie and Joe also hint at predatory or at least carnivorous behavior. Bone marrow is a valuable source of nutrition. My wife, Sara, who has over ten years working in the veterinary industry, pointed out that a normal canine will eat marrow and break bones. The strange aspect of this piece of evidence comes from the location of the bones relative to the depth of the tunnel, and the closed door of the cabin (animals don't close doors) which we mentioned in chapter 8.

The question is often asked of Dogmen (and cryptids in general) why they aren't seen more often, why we don't have proof of their existence, or how they could remain hidden when so many are looking for them? The Land Between the Lakes, and environments like it, could be the answer. Without a unified, organized, scientific effort to locate them, coupled with a lack of belief even within the cryptozoological community, transposed into an environment that provides nigh-infinite food, water and concealment, it may be decades or even a century before we can conclusively say what is or is not Between the Lakes.

Once again, some canines can hear sounds from up to ten miles away. With this in mind, an animal who wants to avoid detection could do so long, long before any human being got within any reasonable distance. It's often speculated that Sasquatch will only be seen if it wants to be seen, and I would argue that the same is true here.

There may be packs of a dozen or more of these creatures flitting about between the trees, who scamper off to more isolated areas as soon as they hear or smell us coming. They would leave trace evidence in the form of scat, scent markers and the scraps of kills - the same as a coyote, wolf or pack of wild dogs. Chasing them on foot would be pointless - wolves can reach nearly 40 miles an hour at a dead sprint. If we make that comparison to a creature which we might assume to be some sort of enhanced wolf, there's no telling how much distance one of these things might cross before a human being gets within a mile of one. A vehicular pursuit might be more effective but would negate any semblance of stealth. And as the rugged, narrow, winding roads of the LBL illustrate, is altogether impossible. This is of course hyperbole - a ravenous pack of large predators would, inevitably, be seen by someone eventually. But what about one, maybe two, or perhaps even a small group or family system?

Were a "dead Dogman" to be discovered, its remains would likely resemble that of a known animal. Decomposition happens very rapidly in the wild, and the LBL is full of scavengers that would have an easy time picking a large carcass clean. Say we discover a "Dogman skull" poking out of the leaves one day - what would differentiate it from that of a wolf, dog, or coyote?

Anecdotes

Martin Groves would describe in detail his encounter with an upright canine, in which he was followed back to his camp by an unseen being before two of the creatures emerged from the woods. The creature seemed to stalk him for several hours.

Jessi and Joe Doyle would describe being observed from the trees by a large beast with pointed ears. They discovered the creature after responding to a heavy rustling in the bushes and found the silhouette of the animal in an area entirely separate from the commotion. My first thought upon hearing this story was that there may have been two of the creatures - one to observe, and one to distract, but this is only speculation.

Another encounter which I was unable to verify and therefore did not explore in detail concerns a couple camping by the side of Lake Barkley. A third witness would see a large animal emerge from the trees and set upon the couple, and, depending on the variation of the story, they did not survive. Both Martin Groves and Elijah Henderson would mention this incident during our interviews.

The story of the Massacre is entirely centered on a direct attack by one or perhaps two of these beings. During his interview with the Cryptid Studies Institute, Roger mentions that two of the victims were, or may have been, bitten on the neck. This is a common hunting tactic for wolves, as we have discussed. Canines will also "play" with a kill, tossing it into the air and slamming it down again, or rearing up on hind legs to stomp a prey animal with the forepaws. I've personally witnessed this behavior in Rottweilers, German Shepherds and Belgian Malinois - breeds which are often mentioned when one attempts to describe the subject of a Dogman encounter. Roger's guess that the animals may have bitten or broken the victim's necks based on what he saw would seem to correlate this.

A purebred domestic Rottweiler. Photo by Marco and Adana Mendoza.

Moving on

In short, several of the anecdotal cases we have explored seem to indicate a pattern of behavior consistent with known canines. Wolves will stalk and surround prey before attacking. They will seize prey by the neck, and even domestic dogs display play behaviors that humans may interpret as cruel, but which are just inherited hunting traits. The environment we have explored also lends itself to the existence of any number of animals, and it may be worth noting that sightings in this area are concentrated in the wild stretches of the park as opposed to nearby population centers. At least, as far as we know right now.

The problem with comparing Dogmen with biological, known canine hunters is that so many encounters seem to bleed into the realm of the bizarre, uncanny and inexplicable.

Instances of what some refer to as mind-speak. Independently glowing eyes. Feelings of not only fear, but pure existential dread. Mysterious clouds of mist and noxious fumes. Hints that these seeming werewolves may be relatives of ancient, evil things our ancestors thought of as being akin to demons. And, of course, the fact that they are walking around upright.

We will soon flip to the other side of the coin and explore the more spectral side of this confounding pattern.

17
The State of The Search

The search for Dogman is an ever-evolving pursuit. Like most aspects of the paranormal world, new reports and evidence trickle in at a steady pace, forcing enthusiasts to continually reassess existing data. My own time spent in the world of Dogman has validated this - since the release of my first book, *The Texas Dogman Triangle*, I've received no fewer than four previously undocumented reports of Dogman appearances within the Triangle itself, rendering my one-time magnum opus, by definition, an incomplete work.

The community is a large one and growing all the time; the subreddit r/dogman has over 21,000 members at time of writing. It was established in January of 2016 and is a regular haunt for many believers and skeptics. Facebook is home to several Dogman groups, including sub-branches of the NADP (The North American Dogman Project) as well as independent organizations. Some are focused on specific regions while others are more general, but the growth of those interested in this phenomenon is evident (to say the least).

Films

Documentaries have played a large role in spreading the word of Dogman, so to speak, several of which have provided valuable reference points in my own research. The original STM "Werewolf Trilogy" are three favorites - *The Bray Road Beast, Skinwalker: Howl of The Rougarou* and *American Werewolves*, specifically. Well known podcaster Tony Merkel, host of the long running *Confessionals Podcast*, along with director Ward Hiney of Dark Holler Films and filmmaker Christian B. Roper appeared in the 2022 film *Expedition Dogman*. Ward Hiney would go on to direct *Werewolves Unearthed*, focusing on Dogman-like activity in Pennsylvania in 2023. 2022 also saw the release of *Dogman Tales* from director Jeremy Norrie.

I might cringe at too much self-promotion, but I was fortunate enough to appear in the adaptation of *The Texas Dogman Triangle* (*The Dogman Triangle: Werewolves in the Lone Star State*), alongside Shannon Legro (and several of my other Fortean role models) which was also released in 2023. The upcoming (at time of writing) film *Dogman Territory: Werewolves in The Land Between the Lakes* was filmed during the research phase of this book and serves as a spiritual successor to *The Dogman Triangle*.

We have already mentioned the film *Hunt the Dogman: High Strangeness in Kentucky* from author and investigator Barton Nunnelly. *The Werewolf Experiments* series and accompanying videos produced by Hellbent Holler are an invaluable documentation of true Dogman fieldwork, and the YouTube series *The Manwolf Files*, hosted by Eli Watson and Karac St. Laurant, provides a documentary-style overview of several different cases from a historical and scientific standpoint. Both series are available on YouTube. For the sake of full disclosure (and self-promotion) the author appears in Season 2 of *The Manwolf Files*, set to premiere before this book goes to print.

Podcasts

The world of paranormal podcasting, where I cut my own teeth as an introduction to my current life as a paranormal researcher, is dominated by Dogman-centric episodes and, in some cases, entire programs devoted to our upright walking query.

Dogman Encounters Radio, hosted by Vic Cundiff, has been running since 2014 and boasts almost 500 published episodes (493 at time of writing). Josh Turner, host of the popular show *Paranormal Roundtable*, regularly discusses the Dogman topic with such vehemence that he has been awarded the nickname "Wolf" by many of his fans and followers. Jeremiah Byron of *The Bigfoot Society* podcast has recently begun digging into the topic, featuring interviews with, among others, Martin Groves, Darrell Denton and even myself. These are but three prominent examples in a very deep pool, and the reader is encouraged to type "Dogman" into the search field of their favorite podcatcher for additional programs. Likely more are being produced as we speak.

Books

We may argue that Dogman fever started with books. Specifically, the works of Linda Godfrey, which are almost universally heralded as the best writing on the subject matter. Linda's books brought the Dogman phenomenon into the limelight, and no fewer than four of these were referenced during the research phase of this volume.

We have made frequent reference to Sabine Baring-Gould's *The Book of Werewolves*. Montague Summers would publish *The Werewolf in Lore and Legend* in 1933. Authors such as Joedy Cook, DA Roberts, Ken Gerhard, Nick Redfern, Barton Nunnelly and Lyle Blackburn, among others, have written a breadth of volumes on the subject. The late Rosemary Ellen Guiley, who penned 49 books on the strange, occult and supernatural published *The Encyclopedia of Vampires, Werewolves and Other Monsters* in 2004. Josh "Wolf" Turner, mentioned only a moment ago, published *Werewolves and the Dogman Phenomenon* in 2023. Even the great John Keel, whose work laid the foundation for most of what I do with my time in 2023, made mention of *La Bête du Gévaudan* in the 1970 book *Strange Creatures from Time and Space*. *La Bête* is covered far more empirically in *Beast: Werewolves, Serial Killers and Man Eaters - The Mystery of the Monsters of The Gevaudan* by Gustavo Sanchez Romero and SR Schwalb. My own meager offerings notwithstanding, there is a healthy and growing library of literature available to the intrepid Dogman researcher. The examples mentioned here represent only what I can see presently occupying my bookshelf. By the time anyone reads this, the aforementioned list will likely already be missing several more titles.

"Evidence"

From time to time, a video of a large, bipedal creature will surface online purporting itself to be evidence, at long last, of Dogman's existence. They are without fail blurry, shot from far away and leave the viewer to interpret whether they are looking at a large dog, man in a suit, or in some cases, nothing at all. Admittedly there aren't a whole lot of them, versus the bigfoot community in which a new video seems to surface roughly every fifteen standard minutes, but there are several to be found. Only two videos have come to my attention which I vaunt as un-debunkable at present - one can be seen in *The Dogman Triangle: Werewolves in the Lone Star State*, and the other was shared with me by Joedy Cook of the NADP. In both cases these videos found their way to my inbox through private channels, and I have since been unable to locate them online.

Audio recordings are an interesting category; I've heard a few which forced me to stop and take stock. While speaking with Tex Wesson, host of the podcast *Tex's Front Porch*, in 2022 during an interview for *The Dogman Triangle*, he shared an audio clip with myself and the production team of what might easily serve as the howl of any Hollywood werewolf. It's not an exaggeration to say it gave me chills. Detractors will immediately decry the audio as too clear or easily hoaxable, but Mr. Wesson is not known for rampant hyperbole or circulation of falsehoods. Quite the contrary, as a matter of fact.

The North American Dogman Project contains three audio files recorded in different parts of Ohio, a purported hotbed of Dogman encounters.

It must be admitted, however, that often the available alleged evidence does not stand up to scrutiny. Eli Watson, co-host of *The Manwolf Files*, would offer the following statement when I asked for a ballpark percentage of hoaxes vs. compelling evidence in the niche.

"In the cases of Dogman evidence that I have examined, the vast majority of them were provable hoaxes. About 90% of them, were either misidentified animals with mange, or some were stills taken from older werewolf movies and more still outright fabrications. In fact, I have come across more outright photoshopped hoaxes than anything else, leaving the evidence pool for Dogman severely lacking."

Karac St. Laurant, founder of Crash Course Cryptozoology and creator of *The Manwolf Files*, would offer a similar response,

"Out of all the photographs, pieces of footage, footprints, all those sorts of examples of alleged evidence, I have found that an astronomically large percent are provable hoaxes in one way or another. For the past few years, I've really been exposing myself to Dogman forums and pages, and I've dedicated a lot of time to tracking down pieces of evidence. You have some really popular examples that are provable hoaxes, like the Gable film or what I call the 'barnyard' photograph, the latter of which is actually the easiest one to disprove. The Gable film's photographer came forth and demonstrated how it was made, which itself takes some real effort. The barnyard photograph, though? All that required was a reverse-image search on Google, and within five minutes of having found the photograph, I found an earlier version of the same photograph that had no Dogman in it. In short, it was a photograph completely unrelated to Dogman that someone had photoshopped a Dogman into. That is just one, and probably one of the more well-known examples. I could not even begin to tell you, in detail, about every example without accidentally writing a book myself."

An overwhelming deluge of zoomed-in photos adorned with red circles find their way to my news feed more often than anything else. Many online discussion groups are so inundated with these photos that the sheer volume makes detailed examination and commentary impossible at present. It would require a dedicated period of several weeks, by my estimation, to suss out any potentially viable items. The great majority of them, sadly, seem to be cases of apophenia and pareidolia, if not hoaxes themselves, as discussed by Eli and Karac above.

Compelling photos and casts of footprints are, once again, in short supply, but have been documented. One was captured by Mike Smith, whom we have already met, and he graciously agreed to its inclusion in this book. Again, to the discussion groups of the online community, footprints are nearly as common as zoomed-in patches of brush captioned with "do you see it?" but many I've examined are almost certainly that of humans, dogs and even feline culprits such as bobcats and cougars. Plenty are also just regular sized sequences of what are probably dog prints, sometimes purported as "a juvenile Dogman running on all fours left these," or something similar. We need not deconstruct the problems with this idea (it's probably just a dog).

Hoaxes

The difficulty in examining evidence often comes from our inability to validate its authenticity. Sources are another aspect of these cases which are in short supply. Where does this clip, image, audio file originate? The absence of a source is always a red flag, but fortunately the internet provides enough hard research tools to at least get us started.

Still images from video games, films and TV shows overlain onto real-world photographs are a recurring trend, as Eli mentioned a moment ago. Sometimes a reverse image search will do the trick in sussing them out, but this is only so effective. It generally takes the informed eye of someone familiar with the source media to make the catch, and there are only so many hours in the day one can devote to watching werewolf movies (or so I'm told).

In recent months, the use of AI imagery has dramatically altered the field of paranormal research. It must be emphasized that the technology has evolved very rapidly, from a high sci-fi concept available only to multi-billion-dollar companies and genius-level programmers to a cottage industry that has placed AI art generators in the hands of every person with access to the internet. "I know Photoshop" was once the graphical design equivalent of a black belt in the martial arts, and while there's no substitute for human creativity, some tasks which were once highly specialized can now be achieved with a few strokes of the keyboard.

I recently plugged a few prompts into an AI video generator as an experiment while pondering this exact topic. I asked the generator to produce "Bigfoot crossing a bridge in the woods chasing a dog."

The resulting clip was not an exact match to my request but did superimpose a bipedal silhouette emerging from the woods near a footbridge. Instead of being chased, the dog I requested stood on the bridge and watched the "sasquatch" as it crossed the adjoining path. It was hardly a convincing video but contained many of the hallmarks of alleged cryptid evidence found online. Blurry, making it difficult to identify edits or airbrushing. Far enough away to deny a clear look but still enough to make one think of something not-quite-human. Nothing in frame to indicate the time, place, or date. The added touch of the dog *responding* to the superimposed image was probably the most striking detail, one which I assumed would be difficult to fake. It wasn't. Bigfoot even had a shadow that perfectly tracked its movement.

We have just entered a phase in the paranormal world where we *must* critique any potential visual evidence based on its emergence relative to the widespread availability of AI image and video generators. UFOs, Ghosts, Bigfoot, Dogman, Sky Squids - given a free afternoon, virtually anyone now has everything they need to make their very own compelling and viral "evidence."

We are far from the end of this discussion, and too near to the beginning for further analysis. Perhaps I'm wrong and there won't be a deluge of AI generated "evidence" polluting our social media feeds in the coming years.

I don't think that I am.

Liars

Fraudulent eyewitness reports are (probably) the biggest issue, coupled with the anonymity of the internet. Anyone can literally say anything at any time. The problem here is that we have zero means by which to flag a story as true, and no clear metric by which to judge it as a fabrication. We can look for common threads which correlate to other Dogman encounters, and we can apply basic human logic and try to determine if the details of a story are too outlandish to be believed. Were either of these sufficient, however, this book would have no reason to have been written.

As we've seen, highly credible witnesses can have highly bizarre encounters. The "caliber" of a story's weirdness does not indicate whether it should be considered as reality. Perhaps the only metric we have in the Dogman world, and really, in any study of the inexplicable, comes from our ability to vet the witness themself, save the rare case where physical evidence is presented (which, as we've seen, presents an entirely different set of challenges).

Anonymous internet reports do not provide us this opportunity. We're left with a much smaller section of analyzed reports made by non-anonymous and credible witnesses to compare less verifiable stories alongside, but even this approach dwells purely in the realm of speculation. We can *assume* that a report which is left in the comment thread of a random forum post from 2004 on a Bigfoot website describing an apparent werewolf is not someone making up their own story after hearing about the Beast of the LBL, but we can never be sure. This is a hypothetical example.

I will say that I have rarely interviewed any seeming Dogman witnesses who I did not find credible based on their demeanor, background, occupation, interest or place within the paranormal niche, location and date of their sighting, and any other criteria I could think to measure their story against. In some cases, a report has come my way which even I was hesitant to consider "valid," but again we run into the issue of the researcher trying to define what the research should entail, instead of simply gathering data and presenting it without bias.

I will state on the record that those interviewed for both of my presently published books are people I consider credible, and their contributions to these works are appreciated beyond the breadth of a simple "thank you."

Separation of Terms

The reader may have taken notice of the fact that the terms "Dogman" and "werewolf" are used interchangeably in this volume, as it was pointed out implicitly in Chapter 4. This is done intentionally, for reasons examined below, but to acknowledge that this verbiage is confusing is an appropriate component to this discussion. Defining these terms as they are generally accepted and perhaps offering an explanation as to why some do or do not consider them synonymous, is our next task. (Outside, of course, the necessity of avoiding repetitive language as much as possible - including this sentence, Dogman/Dogmen appears exactly 260 times within the body of this book [not counting the title], whereas Werewolf/Werewolves is found 94 times.)

Werewolf is, of course, the older of the two terms. It is the one used most colloquially in modern society, and the one which every person you've ever met has heard at least a few times. This is inescapable, as the moniker is so intimately woven into pop culture.

The term is a compound word, descended from the old English *"werwulf"* and derived from older German dialects. The phonetic *"ware"* in the word translates to "man," with *"wulf"* as an obvious preceptor or "wolf." Its popular use originates in the 15th century and has not left humankind since. It generally conjures images of black magic, ancient curses and shapeshifting monstrosities, and your average layperson is not likely to make an immediate connection to cryptozoological phenomena upon hearing it.

Again, referencing Chapter 4, this age-old moniker is often used by apparent Dogman witnesses when describing the subject of their encounter. There is a tendency on the part of some in the research community to point out that "werewolves aren't real" and "Dogmen are real cryptids," which seems unwilling to acknowledge that the entire basis of this search is built on eyewitness testimony. Where our right, as researchers, comes from to say to a witness "no, what you saw was this, it's called that," remains a mystery to me.

Scanning the comment threads of announcement media for *Dogman Territory: Werewolves in the Land Between the Lakes* and *The Dogman Triangle: Werewolves in the Lone Star State* (as two examples) has made this evident. While I don't know if director Seth Breedlove did so intentionally, placing both Werewolf and Dogman in the titles of these films provided an interesting cross section of opinions as to their differences.

"Dogman" of course emerged much more recently, spreading far and wide due in no small part to the work of Linda S Godfrey. It's a simple label, speaking directly to the nature of the beast in question, an almost no-frills descriptor which can conjure only so many variations. It makes sense - much like the issue of the Chupacabra and the Texas Terror Dog, it's often prudent to adopt separate descriptors for the sake of clarity. If we are, in fact, discussing a flesh and blood cryptid and not a supernatural entity, then we of course should define them as separate creatures.

But all that aside, that the etymological roots of werewolf and Dogman are essentially the same is inescapable. Re: they pretty much mean the same thing. I have found it simpler and more in keeping with the eyewitness reports I've studied and received not to separate them.

As all this material is subjective, we're left to decide for ourselves whether these names can be used synonymously; I say that they can. Many will disagree, but the continuing analysis of these terms and what they mean contribute to a not-insignificant amount of the ongoing Dogman discussion.

Besides, how do we know that *both* aren't real, occupying separate places in what we perceive as reality? Could there be an unclassified animal that *resembles* a werewolf, while werewolves themselves lurk in separate shadows? And how would we know from an "a-typical" Dogman encounter, when the only specific aspect is that of a bipedal wolf, whether one is seeing a shapeshifter in animal form or an animal in its mundane form?

Where Does One Go?

During our interview with Jessi and Joe Doyle, Joe relayed a quick summary of a report he received out of North Carolina during the earlier deluge that had prompted the team to embark on their "Dogman Summer" expedition.

A man in his car was chased by an upright, canine-like form, and not knowing where else to go, reached out to a well-known Bigfoot sighting reporting group. The sighting was apparently discarded by the agency, as the physical characteristics were not "a-typical" enough of other Sasquatch encounters. An interesting point here is that a group dedicated solely to Sasquatch research seemed to believe that this encounter did not constitute a "sasquatch misidentification," as is the assumption in many of these cases.

A quick and incomplete list of a few of the groups involved in Dogman research was mentioned above. I believe any person or group that sets out to investigate this creature or even has a passing interest deserves a place at the proverbial table, but this does present us with yet another interesting obstacle.

When one has a werewolf encounter, where does one go? How do you know who is reputable, who will take you seriously, who will protect your privacy, and who will not take your story and spin it to suit their own agenda?

Some are reticent to speak with any kind of researcher at all, preferring to keep their stories private. Several witnesses are mentioned in this book who sat on their own encounters for many years, sharing them only when the appropriate climate presented itself.

In addition, data is not always or often shared between these groups. I have done some small amount of work in trying to compile reports from different sources, and the initial result of this work was the naming of *The Texas Dogman Triangle*. I had an advantage in that Texas was, at that time, not often discussed in widespread discussion of Dogman phenomena, thereby limiting the pool of encounters in a way that indicated (to me) an absence of fraudulent claims. In the Land Between the Lakes, as well as other known hotbeds such as Ohio, conjecture over the subject has been around for a lot longer, and plenty of whackos have had plenty of time to inject unverifiable claims into the water supply. A comprehensive database, on par with the BFRO's annals of bigfoot reports, or the NUFORC UFO sighting archive, is not present in the Dogman world. The NADP has made great strides, and their website is a frequent point of reference for myself and many others, but quite a few reports have come to my attention that were simply never sent to the database's administrators.

The existence of such a database would allow us to cross reference reports with much greater ease. Data points for dates would yield a tremendous amount of insight. If a single claim was received, say, right before the world premiere of the first *Underworld* movie, it could be considered more viable than a torrent of reports rolling in the weekend that the film showed up in theaters. And what about lunar cycles, weather patterns, adjacency to holidays, mineral compositions of the area in question, or even the percentage of reports which correlate based on Dogman's eye color, musculature, or fur coverage?

The work done by the Olympic Project in the Sasquatch world provides something of an ideal parallel. The Olympic team has been gathering empirical data in an apparent Sasquatch hotbed for sixteen years, at the time of this writing. Their research is not limited purely to apparent or even suspected Sasquatch evidence in the Olympic Peninsula, but also the surrounding area and the natural environment. Chris Spencer, the group's ad-hoc audio specialist, has examined numerous examples of what may be Bigfoot vocalizations echoing through the woods, some inaudible until played back after recording. Many more hours and hundreds more gigabytes have been spent cataloging the vocalizations of known animals in the area, providing a database through which potential evidence can be cross referenced.

This kind of work is difficult, time consuming and does not attract the clout that many are inclined towards chasing. It is also expensive, and there are few in the modern day who can abandon their day jobs and spend ten hours a day doing hard research in the woods. Even the members of The Olympic Project balance their work with the necessities of full-time employment.

Perhaps, someday, a Tom Slick-esque millionaire will take to financing Dogman research and hire a few of us on. Let this chapter serve as the cover letter to my own application.

Politics

Divisions and disagreements present additional challenges. Like the problem described above, organizations splitting off from one another or leaders going their separate ways generates additional time/energy sinks, distracting those most interested and best equipped to research the phenomenon. Like a restaurant losing half of its core staff, Dogman research groups seem plagued by a revolving door of divisive dialog.

In the last year, accusations of plagiarism, fraud and even doxxing have dominated the comment threads of many large discussion groups. Some implied threats of violence have even been brought to my attention. I count myself extremely fortunate to have succeeded in avoiding much of the community's controversy during my tenure within it, even canceling a scheduled AMA for my first book after a quick perusal of other discussion threads within the same group revealed that the event was not likely to benefit my career or mental health. Call me a coward, but I slept better after making the decision.

This is hardly a new occurrence in the paranormal world, or in any community for that matter. I found myself on the losing end of a flame war on a popular *Godzilla* forum shortly after the dawn of the new millennium, and this was in a group entirely devoted to the discussion of films featuring actors in rubber suits stomping on cardboard buildings. This is a tongue-in-cheek comparison, made to illustrate that human nature will usually find a way to divide us when passions run high. For many involved in the search of upright canines, this phenomenon is extremely real, and in many cases, deeply personal. It should come as no surprise that disagreement is a component, but one does have to wonder what could be achieved in a more unified - and better financed - field.

18
Travel Log #3 - Fear is the Mind Killer

11/4/23
10:27 PM CST

We've just visited the site of Martin Groves' initial encounter in 1993. It's an isolated area, which would go without saying given where we are, but this location is thick with a sense of deep isolation.

Off the main road, down a bumpy dirt and gravel path long overgrown with tall grass. The Jeep rocks and jostles as we reach a dead end, slowing to a halt just behind Martin's truck. My wish to experience the Breedlove Mobile's off-roading capabilities has come true.

Martin leads us on foot from here - passage by vehicle is no longer possible.

We come to a place nestled deep in a dry gully. On one side the rock and dirt wall, decorated by roots and pitted with notches, hovers overhead to at least my own height plus half. On the other side, the gully gives a slow rise to a slope which must climb at least fifty to seventy-five feet up, though the distance is difficult to gauge in the dark. The leaves are ankle deep, like other areas we've visited. And, once again, it's dark - the darkest it's been in the woods yet during our visit, perhaps reiterating the remoteness of our present coordinates. Occasionally someone will trip over a half-buried tree branch or catch a low hanging one to the forehead. Martin seems the only one unperturbed, not slowing even when a claw-like limb rakes across his face, narrowly missing his eyes. As we proceed, he asks that we limit the range of our own flashlight beams to exclude his line of sight, explaining that he can get around easier using his own night vision. He soon gives proof of that claim, outpacing the rest of our party with the minor aid of a walking stick.

Martin recounts his 1993 encounter much as he did during our interview that same afternoon. His tone is as measured and steady as ever, but there is a noticeable difference in the way his eyes scan our surroundings.

If anything, he is more alert. More vigilant.

"This is the place," he says simply, gesturing about to indicate the approximate location of his tent and campfire. He recalls the mortal terror he experienced that night, after being stalked through the woods by a red-eyed creature moving on two legs. He recounts the flight from the camp, and the ensuing chaos as a pair of apparent werewolves lay waste to it. He discusses mind-speak, saying frankly that the thing he saw meant to do him harm, and communicated that intent directly into his own thoughts. He describes a paralytic feeling of terror and regaining his faculties only after calling for aid in the form of prayer. I can't help but think of a line from *Dune,* my favorite book, penned by Frank Herbert almost sixty years ago to the date.

"Fear is the Mind Killer."

Martin then directs our attention to the hill, above which the line of the sky is barely discernible.

"That's the site of three Native American burial mounds."

I can't help but stare into the blackness. I've been asked more than once if my own research correlates the location of burial mounds with Dogman encounters. Given that pretty much all of Texas was once Native American or Mexican land and that most of my study has been centered there, I've answered with simply, "I don't know."

Now it does. Now, what Linda Godfrey noticed and researched over a decade ago has leapt out of the woods at me. It's no longer an interesting anecdote - it's a recurring correlation.

We turn our flashlights off after a few minutes, doing our best to be silent and take in the natural emptiness of the night. In truth, it's anything but empty - the wind rustles the trees, insects and small animals stir in the brush, and the occasional branch snaps in the frigid air. Absent, however, are engine noises, the sounds of stereos and Bluetooth speakers, and human voices (save our own). Absent are any ambient sources of light other than the moon and stars. Most absent of all, which now becomes strikingly clear in the near blackness, is a place to escape to. A place to hide or seek shelter if a towering creature should choose that moment to lumber out of the underbrush. A wild and theatrical scenario flashes through my mind of our team scattering in all directions, slathering jaws and glowing eyes at our heels. No such creature appears. I unintentionally disrupt the silence by switching on my voice recorder - an older model devoid of a mute function. It chimes as it springs to life. I snatch a small stone from beneath the leaves and slip it into my field pack, intent on adding it to my collection of rocks found in strange places.

Our return hike to the vehicles is as slow as our initial descent down the footpath, and what must have been a thirty-six-point turn was required to avoid rolling the Jeep off the road and into the gully. The hour-long drive back to Cadiz left us with plenty of time to reflect, but it was only the beginning for a writer increasingly out of his depth. I now wrestle with thoughts of what

Martin experienced, how it fits into the larger Dogman phenomenon, and for my own purposes, how to write about it. This is not the first bone chilling Dogman encounter I've studied, but it is the first I've heard while standing on the spot where it happened. Like a ghost tour in New Orleans, but without the ghosts, or the tour. I'll be home in less than thirty-six hours, but I'll carry this place with me indefinitely. Whenever anyone asks why these reports persist when we don't have proof of these creatures' existence, I'll likely point to this place. I'll likely answer, "Because most people don't camp in their hunting grounds."

Martin Groves' 1993 campsite during the filming of *Dogman Territory: Werewolves in the Land Between the Lakes* in 2023. From left to right; Zac Palmisano, Courteney Swihart, Aaron Deese, Shannon LeGro, Martin Groves. Photo by Seth Breedlove.

19
On the Spectral Side

"Dogmen do seem bound by at least some of our natural laws while they are here and choosing to interact with us. Are they 'from here' though? Raised in dens with a mom and pop? Taught how to hunt, hide, or terrorize people when the situation calls for it? I don't believe so. Dimensional interlopers, portal jumpers, conjurings from a curse gone wrong? (or right) All I know for sure, is catching the attention of one shouldn't be on your bucket list."
Shannon LeGro

There is quite a lot one must consider when pondering the state of strangeness in the Land Between the Lakes. It can result in hours of rabbit-hole investigation online, endless field work and potentially days of eyewitness interviews without giving one a comprehensive or satisfactory place to hang their proverbial hat. Having undertaken this task to complete the aforementioned list, I can attest to this personally. Here we will attempt to parse out and ponder the assorted phenomena within and adjacent to the park and examine their potential relation to the more bizarre aspects of the Dogman phenomenon.

During our interview with Jessi and Joe Doyle on the topic of Dogman encounters they'd received, Shannon would ask,

"What about those strange reports that just don't fit 'flesh and blood?'"

"Most of them are strange," Joe replied, "We rarely get that, 'Hey I saw it on the side of the road, eating roadkill, just saw it and it was walking through. The majority of them have extremely strange characteristics."

"There is some kind of a supernatural element to this," Jessi added, "I don't know what it is, but there is no way that this is just a weird product of evolution or something like that. With most of these reports there's something supernatural to it."

Before this exploration is complete, a deeper dive of said supernatural is necessary - and perhaps, overdue.

The Earliest People

The history of indigenous peoples, whose own folklore and belief systems permeated the area long before European settlers set up shop is a factor one truly cannot fully account for. Prehistoric hunter-gatherers were the earliest inhabitants, with fossil records suggesting the presence of nomadic Paleo-Americans as far back as 5-10,000 years ago. Their earliest appearance in the United States proper can be traced to modern day Ohio as far back 13,000 years ago, as they settled into the Cuyahoga Valley after the retreat of the Wisconsin Iceberg near the end of the Ice Age. These were the descendants of big game hunters who contended with ancient megafauna - that is, very large animals - such as the wooly mammoth and mastodon. They would also have thrown their spears against giant ground sloths and sabretooth cats, among others. Post Ice Age humans lived and sought prey here in unknown numbers. As we have examined, the fossil record does not support the idea of an upright canine, but might one of these ancient creatures have provided a template upon which the Dogman archetype was molded?

Native American tribes shared the region as a hunting ground, with some accounts suggesting that the land was owned by the Chickasaw tribe leading into the 1800s. This is mentioned by the official Land Between the Lakes website, which also states that it is not supported by any historical or archeological evidence. Once again, the land served as a source of food and other resources, but for reasons we may not be able to fully ascertain, was not likely a permanent native settlement. What folklores and mythologies sprung from this place and were then lost to history during these early periods? It may be assumed without saying, but we will certainly never know entirely.

The "Native American Question" is often posed when discussions of the Dogman's origin arise. The idea that they may be actualizations of the Skinwalker folklore, or something that native peoples lived alongside is a recurring idea. Did the First Nations have a presence in this area which might provide a tangential link to modern day sightings? Once again, this may be a question which will never yield a satisfactory answer.

An origin story of the Chickasaw people tells of a large, decidedly beautiful white dog which led the wandering tribe to their homeland in modern day Mississippi. The creature is named *Ofi' Tohbi*, which means White Dog, and has evolved to become a symbol of strength, truth, and honor. Hardly a companion to the reportedly malicious entity that is the subject of our search.

Does any of this provide a sufficient linkage to the "Native American Question"? My instincts suggest that it does not. But, if the testimony of Martin Groves is to be believed, then native elders in the area have confirmed at least some of the background of the stories which haunt the LBL as a part of their cultural history. In the absence of documentation, we may cite the testimony of a credible witness, and Martin Groves, as discussed, fits the bill.

Later Settlers into Today

Much later, settlers who established homes here - French, Irish, Swedish and more - brought along their own ideas about the spirit world, and the beings that dwell beyond the veil of reality.

Some of the earliest settlers along the Tennessee/Kentucky border were of French descent. Arriving from neighboring states, they took to the Land Between the Rivers and established homes across the verdant landscape. These would be the ancestors of many of those displaced during the formation of the Kentucky and Barkley lakes.

The French brought a variety of fairy tales to the North American continent. The *Nain Rouge* of Detroit, for instance, is a harbinger of bad luck said to appear before a disaster. For a better-known example of French influence, the story of Cinderella was first penned by Frenchman Charles Parault in 1697. Its presence in the modern day is, of course, quite well established.

Amongst the rich tapestry of folk stories and campfire tales descended from the French is the creature commonly referred to today as the Rougarou. The term "Rougarou" is an adaptation of an older French term which we have already once discussed - *Loup-Garoux*, or of course, the Wolf Man. Sabine Baring-Gould encountered the creature, if only second hand, in 1865, perhaps not knowing that the beast had already crossed the Atlantic and found a second home in North America.

From the bayous of Louisiana came the Rougarou, a colloquial adaptation of *Loup-Garoux* which persists to this day. Examined in documentary films and chattered endlessly about online, the Rougarou is almost a subset of study within the Dogman niche, providing a specific lineage for the werewolf creature which can be traced to Europe and, more specifically, France. As stated, the *Book of Werewolves* provides a wealth of French folktales and anecdotes on the topic.

The Rougarou's nature extends beyond a simple upright walking wolf. In many ways, it may have more in common with the Skinwalker of First Nations peoples than the Hollywood werewolf which so often comes to mind.

The Rougarou is generally regarded as a decidedly malevolent being. Some describe it as a sort of earth spirit or natural guardian - a part of the order of reality which extends beyond our comprehension or understanding. Said to haunt those who are morally dubious, religiously lazy and/or who speak its name aloud, depending on the story in question, the Rougarou would seem to be as much a spiritual being as a cryptozoological one.

One defense against the Rougarou, passed down by generations of Cajun speaking natives of the Louisiana bayou, is to arrange a line of thirteen small stones at the threshold of one's home. The Rougarou, when attempting to enter the house, will be overwhelmed with the compulsion to stop and count the stones before proceeding.

It would seem that mathematics is not the monster's strong suit, as legend claims that the Rougarou is unable to count past twelve. Confounded, the creature will start over at one and give up at twelve an infinite number of times until the sun rises and chases it back to its lair. This is an interesting parallel to the lore of vampires, who are supposed to be unable to enter a home without permission and are also driven to shadowed places when the sun breaks the horizon.

French fur trappers in the Land Between the Lakes seem to have brought the Rougarou along with them. Chatter online of stories shared by these early settlers concerning upright canines has floated about for years, and the testimony of Martin Groves would seem to confirm that such correspondence does exist, retained in the records of the Transylvania Trading Company. Could these early sightings be the result of folklore in the minds of witnesses blending with sightings of known animals? Most certainly. But it is an odd synchronicity - admittedly a term which risks overuse - that a beast so ingrained in French folklore would rise to prominence in the new millennium in an area settled by, amongst others, the French themselves. While they were far from the only people to set up shop Between the Rivers, this may provide another piece of an increasingly layered puzzle.

There is a history of displacement here, of deep held resentment at one's home being snatched away, described in detail in countless anecdotes and written records. It may be that this is one of the most important aspects when considering supernatural phenomena in the area, but I risk getting ahead of myself.

There is a history of death, some disturbingly recent, of crimes committed and lives cut too short. If the accounts of some witnesses - former law enforcement personnel, specifically - are to be considered, then many more deaths than can be found by consulting headlines have also taken place within the park's borders.

Humankind has played a large role in shaping both the landscape and making changes to the local ecology. Species introduced during environmental efforts beginning in the 1930s are still present, many of them extinct native animals which have been reintroduced. The remnants of the area's iron and limestone operations linger still, the construction and operation of which have altered the environment with dramatic strokes. Finally, the flooding of the Land Between the Lakes, earning it the moniker in the first place, reshaped the valley and created the country's largest inland peninsula. No small order and no small impact. Any one of these acts of human intervention would have traceable effects on the native species and plant life, and here they are layered on top of one another.

We now enter the realm of speculation; and nothing hereafter should be considered anything but that. It must be emphasized that the reader is strongly encouraged to form their own take when considering this phenomenon and that the material below is largely a result of my own theorization.

Projections, Minerals

Are these creatures - the LBL Dogmen, if you will - some sort of amalgamated manifestation? Either a projection on the part of the witnesses, or something unleashed on the world because of the area's history? Have supernatural energies in the Land Between the Lakes been stirred so forcefully that beasts from beyond the theoretical veil have entered our reality? Two years ago, I would have said "no" with an adamant resolve and might even have added something about "dying on this hill." After my trip through the corridors of the Texas Dogman Triangle, I was forced to reconsider that assumption.

The idea of the "tulpa" or "thought form" is a popular line of speculation in the paranormal world. Put simply, and with a very limited understanding of the concept, the basic notion is that human beings can project or manifest physical things out into the world around us. Such projections could account for any number of paranormal encounters; and, it has been suggested that Dogmen may be the result of just such a process.

An equally supernatural idea is that these are purely spiritual entities. They may be the ghosts of dead humans, taking on a beastly form in the afterlife for one or more reasons. They may be elemental or guardian spirits; things tied to the earth which have been awakened after centuries of human encroachment.

Then we come to the concept of portals or gateways to other dimensions. Perhaps these are physical entities but born outside of our reality. Things our eyes aren't meant to see, and which, when we do see them, leave us with lasting negative impressions. How they cross over or manifest in our plane of existence is anyone's guess, but at least this theory is somewhat supported by hard science. We know that alternative realities are at least a possibility, but we may never discover the means to visit them.

A "spectral" Dogman sketch based on eyewitness descriptions. Art by Brett Marcus Cook.

It may require a few leaps of faith to make this assumption. A belief in ghosts would certainly help, as well as a propensity to sympathize with the Stone Tape theory of rocks retaining spiritual energies. Speaking of rocks, the supernatural properties of iron and limestone, and perhaps many other minerals, need also be considered. Some open-mindedness over classical folklore would also be a good ingredient, as the centuries-old stories of werewolves paint them as evil, other-worldly and generally zoologically impossible seem to be in play.

What about the UFO element? The Sasquatch presence? The hauntings and whispers of unmarked government vehicles and rumors of coverups?

I am no detective and lack both the intelligence and resources to satisfactorily theorize on how all these elements may interact. I am also not equipped to satisfactorily investigate each separate phenomena in the detail it certainly warrants. I can postulate based only on my own research and experience.

Iron and Mining

Perhaps the legacy of mining in the area plays a role here. After thousands and thousands of tons of iron and limestone were removed from the landscape a literal void was left in the wake of their extraction.

Iron has, for centuries, been believed to contain protective properties. It is said that some Islamic people believed it to be protection against the Djinn, though a discussion on an Islamic message board suggests that these dangerous entities may regard it as an attractant or adornment. It is also said to serve as a repellent against the fae, and traditionally, cemeteries have long been cordoned off with iron fences.

For centuries, iron has been thought by many cultures to be a protective element, warding against unclean spirits. Some researchers speculate that these entities are synonymous with what we think of as "demons," a term which arose often during my trip to the shadowed haunts of the LBL. The idea that all supernatural entities and occurrences are somehow connected, as postulated by John Keel, would seem to align with the recurrence of iron as a defense against the unknown. As we have mentioned, iron mining and refinement were staple industries of the Land Between the Lakes for decades - even centuries.

Limestone adds to the equation. Stone Tape theory originates in the late eighteenth century, during the rise of spiritualism in the United States. A writer and theorist named Charles Babbage would publish work dealing with the concept of spoken words remaining in existence long after they become inaudible to human beings, and the concept would flourish from there. Today it is one of the most hotly discussed paranormal ideas, right alongside Electronic Voice Phenomena and plain old UFO sightings. The Stone Tape theory of haunting states that some minerals have an innate ability to record or channel spiritual energies, perhaps acting as a sort of supernatural thumb drive. Occasionally, by unknown means or perhaps triggered by the presence of living human beings, said figurative drive is opened, and its contents are dumped into the world. The LBL is heavy with limestone, such that the area was once a major exporter of the material, which has a myriad of industrial applications.

Jessi Doyle would provide another insightful take during our conversation, this one specific to this exact topic. She had no way of knowing, at that point, that much of my recent note taking had centered on iron, limestone, and water. Speaking of the LBL, "It's bound in by water. The folklore is that these supernatural entities, these things can't cross water. This area is bounded on three sides by water."

She continued, "They mined this whole area for iron ore. They processed it through the furnaces and then they shipped it down the Cumberland. Iron is used to defend against evil spirits. It's always been that way. They've taken all this iron out of the land. This whole little chunk of land is just free of any kind of protection from anything. It's a constantly bounded, charged area."

Iron has been mentioned repeatedly throughout this volume, and I will now admit that it was to hint at this precise intersection. I was unaware at first draft that some of my fellow researchers had entertained similar ideas. Jessi, however, summarizes the idea in a manner I had not considered - not only had the land's protection been removed, but potential spiritual barriers had been set up on all sides through human interference. Drastic, sweeping, traumatic changes, not just to the landscape itself, but to the people that lived there - or, more accurately, the people who were forced to leave. The Land Between the Lakes may very well be a place of concentrated, *contained* strangeness, charged by generations of death, displacement, and environmental tampering.

Displacement

There is another factor in this equation which seems to intersect with the phenomenon, and it was mentioned in every interview conducted for this book. It is also generally one of the first things a person mentions when explaining the history of the Land Between the Lakes. A recent conversation would enlightenment me to the fact that not only is this factor consistent in the Land Between the Lakes, but that it can be found and historically verified in other areas of concentrated Dogman activity:

Displacement of human populations.

As we now know, there is a deep history of displacement of the local population within the LBL. We may not ever know what early humans lived in or were forced out of the region, but we know for certain that up to 2,000 American families were forcibly removed in the second half of the 20th century. We do know that anger, resentment and grief for what was lost still lingers in the area today, remembered by the survivors and their descendants.

I felt chills when I realized that this is not the only instance where this is true. A more detailed historical examination of the examples below is certainly in order, as is additional data to either confirm or deny if this theory has any true weight. With those qualifiers in mind, consider the following.

Youngstown - 1987

In 1987, Matt Emch, a paranormal researcher by night and professional radio broadcaster by day, encountered a creature closely fitting the profile of the LBL Dogmen. In addition, the encounter took place interestingly close to the date of the campground massacre in the Land Between the Lakes, save that this sighting would take place over five hundred miles away in Youngstown, Ohio.

It was the summer before high school, and Matt was hanging out with three friends his own age, up to generally harmless mischief as most highschoolers are wont to do. Youngstown, OH was once home to a thriving steel mill, but its doors were closed in the early eighties. By 1987, it sat largely abandoned, and it was here that Matt and his friends had gone to hang out for the evening.

A series of square openings sat in the ceiling of the first, second and third floors of the building, allowing one to peer down into the lower levels from above, and vice versa. It also served as an improvised chimney, and Matt's group lit a campfire beneath the opening to illuminate the darkened space. It was shortly after this that things took a turn.

A large, upright walking form entered the building. It towered over the teenagers, and Matt estimates that it was at least ten feet in height. It stalked with intention across the concrete floor. It drew close to the blazing fire and extended an over-long arm and what Matt describes as a raccoon-like hand toward the flames. An interesting detail is that the creature's palms had a white stripe or slash which stood out against its otherwise dark coat. The flames also seemed to respond to the creature's touch, extending toward its clawed fingers.

"Its arms were so long the fingers could have scratched its ankles standing up straight," Matt explains.

The creature lingered for a moment before ascending a nearby stairwell towards the second floor. Matt's group, dumbstruck by fear and disbelief, were trapped on the third floor of the building as the creature approached. They would escape that night, but the encounter would linger with the four boys well into adulthood. Matt speaks of the encounter today with abject seriousness. Today, he continues to study the paranormal and document his findings and experiences on his YouTube channel, *Planet 412*. This is a very brief summary of his encounter, and readers are encouraged to seek out his testimony in its entirety. He provides a wealth of additional details, including follow-up research conducted in the intervening years to verify the creature's height.

This case is included here for a few reasons. First, and most simply, it fits the profile of many Dogman encounters we've already examined. Second, and perhaps more importantly, it takes place in a defunct steel mill.

Steel operations in Youngstown were big business until a slowdown in the 60s would lead to a complete halt in the early 80s. Thousands lost their jobs, prompting many to leave the area. Youngstown would lose a third of its population by 2022.

Steel, as a quick internet search will reveal, is composed almost entirely of iron.

Iron refinement, displacement of the local population, and Dogman encounters.

Matt's sighting would take place less than three hours' drive from Defiance, OH, which was mentioned early on in this volume as the home of the Defiance Werewolf. It may be that Ohio warrants further investigation on the part of the author, but we must digress for the time being.

These interestingly specific correlations to the Dogmen of the LBL may be just that - correlation. A tangential connection does not prove a common causation, and coincidence is a factor we simply cannot account for. Nevertheless, Matt's story, in addition to being a striking and terrifying case, presents oddly specific parallels to the Dogman activity on the Tennessee/Kentucky border.

We must again return to Wisconsin, where The Beast of Bray Road once walked and may linger to this day. Linda Godfrey noted in her books, including *Real Wolfmen: True Encounters in Modern America,* that sightings are often adjacent to lands once owned by Native American Tribes. This includes a close proximity to known burial mounds. The displacement of Native Americans by later settlers is well documented.

We must also point to Texas, where much of my prior research has been centered. Most, if not all, of Texas once belonged to the First Nations. It may not be possible to know who was pushed out from where in every case, but it does not require too great a stretch to see that this is another area wherein local people have been displaced. Plum Creek, found in the town of Lockhart is one known example, as the lands surrounding it were historically home to members of the Comanche tribe. Battles between the Comanche and European-descended settlers are a dark period of Lockhart's history. The Beast of Plum Creek would allegedly slaughter cattle in the area in the late 20th century.

Displacement. Removal. Families uprooted from their homes. Lives meticulously built from the ground up, laid to waste by greater powers through violence and attrition in the name of "progress."

This is not meant to be a political commentary, but it is a known anecdote that moving house is one of the most stressful things a human being can do. It is often equated with divorce, chronic illness, and death. To be forced into this stressful situation beyond one's control is another realm of strife entirely. Do some energies created by these repeated displacements exist in these areas, and if so, are they a factor in the Dogman's continued appearances?

Even the Chickasaw story of the White Dog is set against the backdrop of the tribe's displacement. Great care must be given in study of these topics not to appropriate or misinterpret Native mythologies to suit one's agenda, and it is mentioned here with this caveat.

We might imagine the situation as such: take a metal box, perhaps two feet by two feet by two feet. You drop in some leaves, some scraps of paper, a shred of cardboard, some small sticks. Every few items you add a dash of lighter fluid - not a lot, just a splash. It soaks into the debris, invisible, but never gone. When the box is nearly full, you place it next to an oven, or a space heater, or even an open flame.

The Peninsula is the box. The history is the kindling, and the lighter fluid, the death and displacement of countless people across multiple generations. What sparks the flame is anyone's guess.

Is Dogman the fire or the ashes it leaves behind?

20
Travel Log #4 - Miles to Go Before I Sleep

11/6/23
7:17 PM EST

A breakfast of coffee, leftover Subway from the night before and too many cigarettes kick off the morning of our departure. Seth orders breakfast from a local diner, but I'm a sucker for leftover Subway. I keep saying I'm going to quit smoking, and I am, but I'd like to finish this book first. You've got to pace yourself.

We concluded the previous evening with a final on-camera discussion, attempting to summarize what we'd experienced over the last two days. The supernatural aspects of the Dogman question are picked apart, as are the rumors of conspiracy and the dozen or more anecdotal encounters we've received in a staggeringly short time. In truth, a comprehensive breakdown is difficult - every approach seems to hint at another, and it becomes impossible to take in the full breadth of what we've learned. At least for me.

What I can say is that the Dogmen of the LBL are nothing if not pedigreed. Whether their lineage is imagined, superimposed by speculation, or whether there is a direct connection to ancient literature, native peoples and/or the settlers of the 1700s, there is much in the past to think on when trying to find some sort of precedent. A proper historical analysis is something I fear I am unequipped to undertake, but I'll at least give it a go. I know more today than I did when I got here.

I make a few last-minute voice notes, and the crew gathers for a final group photo before loading into our respective vehicles. It's been a fun trip, and I can't help but nurse a pang of mourning that it's come to an end.

Aleks drops Shannon and I off at the airport before continuing to film an upcoming episode of *On the Trail of Bigfoot*. The conversation on the road is light, consisting mostly of our colorful dining experiences during the trip, helicopters, and other small talk. I doze off a few times, trying to suppress the urge to work on this exact text. I'll spend the intervening hours in the airport doing just that, and at present, I can't find my air pods.

Layovers and flight times result in a nine-hour trip home, and I devote at least half of it to reviewing notes and digging through *The Book of Werewolves*. It was during this time that I would stumble across the *Rakshasa*, and balance yet another cup of coffee with my notebook on the jump from Nashville to Atlanta.

Attempting to draw conclusions on this journey has proven as impossible as ever. Perhaps I expected answers in the Land Between the Lakes, or perhaps I was just excited to get out in the woods for a little while, but I'm left feeling as if there's something I missed. One or more critical pieces of the puzzle that might paint something of a clearer picture.

I've yet to determine what that is. Perhaps the problem lies in that the Dogman phenomenon, and the saga of the Land Between the Lakes, has yet to reach a conclusion. Perhaps the legacy of all of this, of werewolves and Dogmen, of iron mines and unnatural lakes, of strange places in the woods and displaced populations and so much more, is still being written.

For me, one journey has drawn to a quiet end, but there are leagues yet to cross. I'll set all this aside for a few days after I'm back in San Antonio and spend some time with Sara and Ezra to clear my mind before proceeding. Family is an essential component to the creative process.

Once more I involuntarily invoke Robert Frost, muttering to myself as I step onto the gangway of my final flight.

"Miles to go before I sleep."

21
Conclusions

It should be acknowledged from the start - or the jump, as the kids sometimes say - that the title of this chapter is something of an oxymoron. "Conclusions" are not something we often find in the paranormal field. If true "conclusions" were obtainable, my job would be much easier and much less interesting. To arrive at a notion which is worthy of that moniker requires empirical repeatable data, scientific classification, and the ability to say with complete certainty that this is that, or that is this, or those are certainly these. We can't do that with regards to the Dogman phenomenon, nor the strangeness of the Land Between the Lakes. Nevertheless, an overview of what we have learned and the potential conclusions the data hints at are in order, and so this chapter was named thusly.

At first glance, the Dogman activity within the LBL might seem to be something of an anomaly. While there are other stories of fatal Dogman attacks online, the "LBL Massacre" is the most detailed, the most researched and, as of my trip to the park itself, the most extensively documented. The confirmation by local residents that the story was in circulation as early as 1989

(Mike Smith, Chapter 7) at least precludes the notion that it is an internet creepypasta.

However, a closer look reveals that Dogman sightings in the LBL are not anomalous occurrences, at least not within the "Dogman Universe."

Their appearance, behavior and even chosen environment closely mirrors other encounters I have undertaken to research, resulting in a short list of recurring traits.

- Resistance to gunfire. Two encounters examined in detail here - the notorious "massacre" and the 1993 encounter by Martin Groves - mention the witness (or victim) opening fire on a Dogman-like creature at close range. In these respective cases, the creatures seemed to either shrug off the attack or continue to operate before expiring. Similar stories can be found in Texas, for example, but a quick perusal of a few online message boards yields plenty of additional anecdotes of the same theme. The annals of Dogman literature, which we briefly and incompletely ran down in chapter 17, are riddled with more. A complete list of *Dogmen Who Didn't Mind Being Shot* is not possible here.
- Location. Water in abundance, trees that could conceal an army, a cornucopia of wild

game - all on protected land. Dogmen in general seem to have a propensity for popping up on ranches, desolate roads and national parks and forests. Private, protected spaces which provide plenty of room to hide and hunt. In addition, we have noted that areas which have a history of heavy human displacement seem particularly bothered by these fiendish things. My suspicion, for what it may be worth, is that this is not a coincidence.

- Behaviors. Stalking and staring, attacks and even inflicted fatalities on human beings. The Dogmen of the LBL are described such that they appear to be aggressive, territorial and violent. The profile of potential Dogman activity in the LBL seems (at a glance) to be a touch more grizzly than other concentrated areas which I've studied. While many of their behaviors fall in line with what canines are known to do naturally, they seem to display an awareness and intention that supersedes the intelligence of any classified canine species.

- Witness responses. This is perhaps the most important piece of evidence, and the one I most often cite when trying to describe the nature of these encounters beyond "a wolf on two legs." Overwhelmingly, and with rare exception, experiencers of these uncanny sightings are left unsettled and even disturbed.

Ancient Roots

There is precedent for these characters in some of our oldest mythologies, as discussed in Chapter 5 and other portions of this text. The ancient legends overwhelmingly refer to the Dogmen archetypes as evil (giving exception to the *Wulver*, of course), and the LBL Dogmen are almost universally described as having an evil "presence" about them. I'll once again quote Martin Groves who said,

"A feeling of evil that cannot be described."

There are plenty of examples we did not examine - from the start, I sought to omit the story of King Lycaon of Greek Mythology, referred to by some as the "first werewolf." It seems to arise quite often, and I considered its omission a challenge, but it is included now as an additional point of literary interest.

We can't say if the LBL Dogmen are relatives of the *Loup-garoux*, Rakshasa, Nagual and Skinwalker. We can't say if any or none of these creatures have anything to do with one another, but one would have to ask why, if they are unrelated, they seem to have so much in common. As we saw in their relevant sections, these few examples of shapeshifting human chimera are unique to their respective cultures and time periods but can be commonly described by breaking them down to their very simplest elements - upright wolves. Two legged dogs (The Nagual [Jaguar men] being the exception, though they were said also to be able to transform into wolves).

It indeed seems the phenomenon has been present for a very, very long time. As in Michigan where the Dogman first appeared in 1887, chatter of upright wolves in the LBL is said to originate with the trappers of the Transylvania Company, who began settling the area in the late 1700s.

There is an obvious crossover in the park between Sasquatch and Dogman activity. Some will conclude that witnesses are simply mistaking one for the other, but there's a problem with this idea. We have explored this concept already in detail, but any attempt at conclusions seems to at least lead back in the general direction of this assumption, at least amongst many researchers.

When taking in the whole picture - or at least trying to - one question must be asked. Are the disparate strange occurrences recorded here connected, a part of some grander scheme, or is this simply a place where weird things happen?

Coincidence can't be measured or predicted, but at a certain point coincidence becomes a pattern. Patterns have roots - something must set them in motion. Definite patterns have begun to emerge in the LBL, and may have been present for quite some time, unless we simply take the skeptic's way out and refuse to acknowledge them.

We have examined the history of iron and limestone mining in the park, and some of the supernatural folklore which surrounds them. We have also touched heavily on the topic of displacement and drawn a line along this avenue between various areas that claim repeated Dogman reports. As well, we have touched on the formation of the rivers, the ravaging of the landscape by human enterprise, and attempted to summarize the modern-day hotbed of paranormal activity that the place is. A picture has been painted, but we might liken it more to a jigsaw puzzle with many, many missing pieces.

On Family

A footnote which is of particular interest to me (and likely no one else) is that I have a personal connection to part of LBL's history that was not evident to me until I began actual research into the Transylvania Company, which again is said to have documented the first mention of Dogmen like creatures in what would become the Land Between the Lakes.

My maternal grandmother, whose maiden name was Van Cleave, told myself and anyone else within earshot for many years that we had a distant connection to Daniel Boone by marriage. It was a fun story for an excitable child who always had obtaining a raccoon-tail hat on their to-do list but provided little relevance to my life as I aged. As we learned in chapter 1, Daniel Boone would play a critical role in helping early settlers establish homesteads in the region well before the LBL was ever thought of.

While making notes for this very volume, I ran across a list of Boone's children and their respective spouses. In 1765, Squire Boone, Daniel's son, would marry a woman named Jane Van Cleve. I was quick to note this alternative spelling on the surname but found additional birth and death records for Jane that were a match to my Grandmother's original spelling - Van Cleave. I would love to say that I found an old note written by a distant relative reporting a strange creature on two legs, but such a document has yet to manifest.

My grandmother passed away in 2022, shortly before the completion of my first book. She was an avid supporter of my burgeoning career and reminded me at every opportunity that writing runs in our family (my mother is a published author, and another distant relative is prolific writer Homer Croy, but this is not meant to be an autobiography). To find this familial connection to my current research is, without belaboring the point, a deeply personal synchronicity. Where it fits into the narrative is anyone's guess, but I like to think my Grandmother's legacy is in some way preserved through the existence of this book. It was an odd and enlightening thing to learn that I had spent the last year researching not just the history of Dogmen in Kentucky and Tennessee, but also potentially that of my own family.

What May Matter

It may be that the importance of the Dogman phenomenon lies not in our ability to examine or classify it, but in the people who experience it. The element of these encounters that I find most striking, and that dozens have remarked upon in countless conversations, is that of the response by the witnesses.

Seasoned law enforcement officers, whose trade consists of dealing with the worst of humanity, stricken by decades of nightmares after just one encounter. Lifelong visitors to the LBL, seasoned campers, who avoid certain areas like the literal plague. Distinct and overwhelming feelings of fear and panic. A certainty that one has had a brush with something unnatural.

An eyewitness's recollection of their thoughts and feelings is the only aspect of any testimony which does not rely on the physical description of what a person saw. The height, build and shape of a thing can be misremembered; one's own thoughts and feelings, generally, cannot. Even if these were simple animal sightings, hallucinations or the result of intoxication, the repeatedly negative impressions left on the experiencers leaves us with one essential question - Why?

The reader will find no conclusive answers in this book. I can, however, conclude with a statement of my own opinion, and one which I have found is shared by many others involved in this search.

Werewolves exist, and they live in the Land Between the Lakes.

Citations by Chapter

Chapter 1 - The Introduction

Grand Canyon
https://www.nps.gov/grca/faqs.htm#:~:text=But
%20most%20people%20measure%20the,mile%2
0277%20%2F%20km%20446

LBL About Us
https://landbetweenthelakes.us/about/#:~:text=
As%20part%20of%20America's%20great,in%20W
estern%20Kentucky%20and%20Tennessee

LBL early inhabitants
https://landbetweenthelakes.us/wp-
content/uploads/2022/10/Background-History-
of-LBL.pdf

LBL history summary
https://www.westkentucky.com/history.html

Elk and Bison
https://www.explorekentuckylake.com/lbl/wildli
fe-
viewing/#:~:text=Elk%20and%20bison%20roam
%20free,in%20early%20summer%20and%20fall

March On Washington
https://www.history.com/topics/black-history/march-on-washington

NASA - L Gordon Cooper
https://www.nasa.gov/sites/default/files/atoms/files/cooperl_gordon.pdf
News-Democrat (Paducah, Kentucky) · 23 Aug 1924, Sat · Page 10

The Death of Marilyn Monroe
https://www.latimes.com/local/obituaries/archives/la-me-marilyn-monroe-19620806-story.html

Faces and Stories - The People of the Land Between the Lakes
https://www.youtube.com/watch?v=ePg5BC__sUg

Chapter 3 - Strangeness In and Around

The phantom truck driver and other ghost stuff
https://www.fourriversexplorer.com/land-between-the-lakes-ghosts/

NUFORC sightings database by state
https://nuforc.org/ndx/?id=loc

Mantell Incident

https://www.wkrn.com/news/kentucky/ky-ufo-sighting/

Faces of The Visitors by Kevin Randall (Hopkinsville Incident)

Interview with Jessi and Joe Doyle

Interview with Dewey Edwards

Interview with Jeremiah Byron

Haunted Houses & Family Ghosts of Kentucky by William Lynwood Montell

Pike County Hellhound
https://www.travelchannel.com/shows/mountain-monsters/episodes/kentucky-hellhound-of-pike-county

Boca Del Infierno
https://www.britannica.com/place/Guanajuato-state-Mexico#ref922043

Haunted Places in Guanajuato
https://amyscrypt.com/city/guanajuato/

Strange Places - Lost in the Land Between the Lakes

https://www.youtube.com/watch?v=oBGXTYZQ
C0I&t=907s

Chapter 4 - Dogman: A Profile

The Bray Road Beast -
https://www.onlyinyourstate.com/wisconsin/be
ast-of-bray-road-wi/

The Beast of Bray Road - Linda Godfrey

The Michigan Dogman: Werewolves and Other
Unknown Canines Across the USA - Linda
Godfrey

Defiance Werewolf -
https://astonishinglegends.com/astonishing-
legends/2020/10/11/the-werewolf-of-defiance-
ohio

The Texas Dogman Triangle - Aaron Deese

The Dogman Triangle - Werewolves in the Lone
Star State
Interview with Shannon LeGro

Interview with Jeremiah Byron
The Beast of Bray Road Alive and Well (Eric
Mintel Investigates)

https://www.youtube.com/watch?v=nsvbuj7Siwg

The Bray Road Beast (Film) - Small Town Monsters

Interview with James Witter

The Werewolf Experiments - Hellbent Holler (YouTube)
https://www.youtube.com/watch?v=rDq4C5H_cUI

Chapter 5 - Werewolves Most Ancient

Marduk
https://westportlibrary.libguides.com/marduk#:~:text=Marduk%20was%20the%20patron%20god,storm%20god%20and%20agricultural%20deity

Urudimmu and Pazuzu
https://escholarship.org/content/qt3p25f7wk/qt3p25f7wk_noSplash_6013045d9cb706dfb3fc07646ae120ec.pdf

Baring-Gould biographical information:
https://www.efdss.org/learning/resources/beginners-guides/35-english-folk-collectors/2431-efdss-sabine-baring-gould#

Nagualism
https://www.jstor.org/stable/983361?seq=2#metadata_info_tab_contents

2020 Nagual sighting
https://aldianews.com/en/culture/heritage-and-history/real-nahual-veracruz

Ancient Persian Calendar
https://www.cais-soas.com/CAIS/Religions/iranian/Zarathushtrian/achaemenian_zarathushtrian.htm

https://www.etymonline.com/word/werewolf

The Book of Werewolves - Sabine Baring-Gould

An American Werewolf in London (film)

Flood Myths
https://www.britannica.com/topic/flood-myth

Chapter 6 - The Campsite

Interview with Martin Groves

Chapter 7 - Rumors

Interview with Mike Smith conducted November 2023

The Wampus Cat-
https://science.howstuffworks.com/science-vs-myth/strange-creatures/wampus-cat.htm

Nathan Futrell's Grave-
https://nkytribune.com/2016/07/old-time-kentucky-marker-tells-story-of-youngest-drummer-boy-in-the-war-of-the-revolution/

The Laura Furnace -
https://landbetweenthelakes.us/seendo/self-guided-activites/iron/
LBL Wrangler Trails-
https://www.landbetweenthelakes.us/wp-content/uploads/2015/04/2015LBLWranglersTrailMap.pdf

Chapter 8 - The Thermal

Interview with Jessi and Joe Doyle

The Werewolf Experiments - Hellbent Holler

Faces of The Visitors by Kevin Randle
Kentucky Goblins

Chapter 10 - Chasing the Massacre

How Wolves Kill (neck biting)
https://www.largecarnivores.fi/species/wolf/wolfs-diet-and-hunting-behaviour.html#:~:text=The%20wolf%20kills%20its%20prey,marks%20all%20over%20its%20body.

The Bloodthirsty Beast of the LBL (CSI)
https://www.youtube.com/watch?v=ZYoOc0GCEgI

Witness to Family Attack Comes Forward - Beast of LBL Update (CSI)
https://www.youtube.com/watch?v=0swWLqexkvs

Personal recorded notes during conversations with "Roger"

Interview with Mike Smith

Interview with Eli Watson
Interview with Shannon LeGro

Interview with Jeremiah Byron

Interview with Martin Groves

Interview with Elijah Henderson

Interview with Jessi and Joe Doyle

NADP - Land Between the Lakes Documentary
https://www.youtube.com/watch?v=1VpqIOrgVu
o

Birth of the Internet
https://www.popularmechanics.com/culture/we
b/a43903714/when-was-internet-invented/

Beast of the LBL (book)
Steve Causey

Area weather data - April 7th, 1982
https://www.weatherwx.com/climate-
averages/ky/land+between+the+lakes.html

Chapter 11 - Sasquatch of The Lakes

BFRO report #33322 -
https://www.bfro.net/GDB/show_report.asp?id=
33322 - CADIZ - 2010 while leaving Lake Barkley
State Park

Interview with Mike Smith

Interview with Martin Groves

Interview with Elijah Henderson

Interview with Jessi and Joe Doyle

Bigfoot: Beyond the Trail - Central Kentucky Sasquatch Investigation
https://www.youtube.com/watch?v=KbWk86Au F9Y&t=451s

Chapter 12 - The Fog

Interview with Darrell Denton

Interview with Martin Groves

NUFORC Database

The Book of Werewolves

The Bhagavad Gita

The Mahabharata

Chapter 13 - The Footprint

Interview w/ Mike Smith

Video/photos provided by Mike Smith

Chapter 14 - The Dark

The Beast of LBL - Dark Hollow - Nightmare Nuggets of Cryptid Terror - https://www.youtube.com/watch?v=owFRqglvS_Q&t=11s

Interview with Elijah Henderson

Chapter 15 - The Crossing

Weather records https://www.weatherwx.com/climate-averages/ky/land+between+the+lakes.html

Lunar records https://stardate.org/nightsky/moon https://aa.usno.navy.mil/calculated/moon/phases?date=2023-05-06&nump=50&format=p&submit=Get+Data

Interview with Gabby Henderson - November 2023

Chapter 16 - Hunters

Dog noses https://vcahospitals.com/know-your-pet/how-dogs-use-smell-to-perceive-the-world#:~:text=In%20fact%2C%20it%20has%20be

en,10%2C000%20times%20better%20than%20pe
ople

Wolf Ears
https://wolf.org/original-articles/how-wolves-
use-their-sense-of-hearing-to-engage-the-
world/#:~:text=They%20can%20use%20their%20
triangular,most%20acute%20sense%20after%20s
mell.
Wolf bites
https://wolf.org/wp-
content/uploads/2019/09/wildkids_summer201
9-1.pdf

Wolf running speed
https://nywolf.org/2016/07/how-fast-do-
wolves-run/

Dogs night vision
https://www.petmd.com/dog/general-
health/can-dogs-see-dark

Large scale hog hunts - interview with Jessie and
Joe Doyle

General canine behaviors and anatomy -
interview with Sara Deese

Chapter 17 - State of The Search

r/dogman - https://www.reddit.com/r/dogman/

Rosemary Ellen Guiley - https://en.wikipedia.org/wiki/Rosemary_Ellen_Guiley

Josh Turner's book - https://www.amazon.com/Werewolves-Dogman-Phenomenon-Josh-Turner/dp/B0CFCDTPXM/ref=sr_1_1?qid=1703360564&refinements=p_27%3AJosh+Turner&s=books&sr=1-1&text=Josh+Turner

NADP - https://northamericandogmanproject.com/

STM Live - The Olympic Project and Eli Watson

The Manwolf Files

The Werewolf Experiments
The Book of Werewolves

Vampires Werewolves etc/Rosemary Ellen Guiley

Hunt the Dogman

Expedition Dogman

Werewolves Unearthed

Skinwalker: Howl of the Rougarou

American Werewolves

Bray Road Beast

Dogman Encounters Radio

Paranormal Roundtable

BEAST (Gevudaun/book)

The Olympic Project Website

Chapter 19 - On the Spectral Side

The Chickasaw and the White Dog
https://www.chickasawculturalcenter.com/exper
ience/2023/virtual-exhibits/ofi-tohbi-
exhibit/#:~:text=The%20exhibit%20allowed%20vi
sitors%20experience,what%20is%20now%20cent
ral%20Mississippi.

https://www.native-languages.org/chickasaw-
legends.htm

https://www.palomar.edu/users/scrouthamel/ais130/Lectures/paleoind.htm

https://ohiohistorycentral.org/w/Ice_Age_Ohio

https://www.nps.gov/articles/000/discover-the-paleoindian-people.htm

https://landbetweenthelakes.us/wp-content/uploads/2022/10/Background-History-of-LBL.pdf

Stone Tape Theory
https://hauntedwalk.com/news/the-stone-tape-theory/

Interview with Matt Emch conducted by the Author on 12/7/23

Interview with Jessi and Joe Doyle in November 2023

The Vengeful Djinn by Rosemary Ellen Guiley and Philip J. Imbrogno (book)

Voices from The Tapes: Recordings from The Other World by Peter Bander (book)

Matt Emch's Youtube Channel

https://www.youtube.com/channel/UCk3I3p6M
Urr-RMC_Zmw3WoQ

Islamic discussion on Iron and The Djinn
https://islam.stackexchange.com/questions/764
02/are-jinn-scared-of-iron

Chapter 21 - Conclusions

Jane Van Cleave Boone
https://www.findagrave.com/memorial/6755980
2/jane-boone

www.ingramcontent.com/pod-product-compliance
Lightning Source LLC
Chambersburg PA
CBHW022047020426
42335CB00012B/587